How to Keep
SWINGING
WHEN YOU'VE TAKEN MORE HITS THAN A LOUISVILLE SLUGGER

How to Keep
SWINGING
WHEN YOU'VE TAKEN MORE HITS THAN A LOUISVILLE SLUGGER

A guide to help you step up to the plate of life everyday!

RONALD MOORE

LIFE HAPPENS

Tate Publishing & *Enterprises*

TATE PUBLISHING
& Enterprises

Tate Publishing is committed to excellence in the publishing industry. Our staff of highly trained professionals, including editors, graphic designers, and marketing personnel, work together to produce the very finest books available. The company reflects the philosophy established by the founders, based on Psalms 68:11,

"THE LORD GAVE THE WORD AND GREAT WAS THE COMPANY OF THOSE WHO PUBLISHED IT."

If you would like further information, please contact us:
1.888.361.9473 | www.tatepublishing.com
TATE PUBLISHING & Enterprises, LLC | 127 E. Trade Center Terrace
Mustang, Oklahoma 73064 USA

How to Keep Swinging When You've Taken More Hits Than A Louisville Slugger
Copyright © 2007 by Ron Moore. All rights reserved.
This title is also available as a Tate Out Loud product.
Visit www.tatepublishing.com for more information

No part of this publication may be reproduced, stored in a retrieval system or transmitted in any way by any means, electronic, mechanical, photocopy, recording or otherwise without the prior permission of the author except as provided by USA copyright law.

All scripture quotations are taken from the New American Standard Bible ®, Copyright © 1960, 1962, 1963, 1968, 1971, 1972, 1973, 1975, 1977, 1995 by The Lockman Foundation. Used by permission. All rights reserved.

The opinions expressed by the author are not necessarily those of Tate Publishing, LLC.

Book design copyright © 2007 by Tate Publishing, LLC. All rights reserved.
Cover design by Rusty Eldred
Interior design by Lynly D. Taylor

Published in the United States of America

ISBN: 978-1-5988678-0-X
07.05.01

DEDICATED TO

Mr. Bob Duane, who during my "Dark Days of Dallas," when I had made such a mess of my life and "knew for certain" that I had experienced my last chance to step up to the plate at bat, put his hands on my shoulders, looked me in the eyes and squared off at me with, "Ron, God's got *great* plans for you!" During this period of being "benched," I certainly did not believe in me and neither did anyone else that I knew of. Yet in the purest sense, Bobby continued to believe in the Jesus who indwelt my life, knowing that He would discipline me, continue to train me, and motivate me to *keep swinging* in this game of life.

Special Thanks

To my good friend and recording artist, the Story Teller himself, Mr. Layton Howerton and his song "Louisville Slugger" that played a *huge* part in the inspiration for this book.

FOREWORD

The book you are about to read is one that will challenge and inspire you in every way. Ron Moore was a teenager in Oklahoma City when I served as pastor in that area. I got to know him and quickly saw that he had a heart for God and a drive to make a difference in the world. I have watched him through those maturing years, further experiences in the Marine Corps, success and struggle as a pastor, the break-up of his home and the rebuilding of his life and family. It is an incredible journey that he has been on.

Through it all he has maintained his strong commitment to his calling as a Christian and his vision of making a difference in the world. His experiences are things that many of you reading these pages have been through, are going through or will go through. He opens his heart and shoots straight about his life and what God wants for all of us. You will laugh and cry as you read through his pilgrimage and will be challenged to keep getting up when you are knocked down. That is the difference in people in this world. Everyone gets knocked down. Not everyone gets up.

These pages will help you know the key to facing all of the challenges of life and emerge stronger, happier and more fulfilled because of the struggle. It is an easy read, but a must read for all.

Dr. Jimmy Draper

President Emeritus, LifeWay Christian Resources

July 2006

INTRODUCTION

All of us take certain "hits" in life. Some are deserved, some are not. But when you realize that pain is pain whether a person deserves it or not, it helps greatly in dealing with the "no-duh, truth," that pain hurts! Oh yes, whether we bring the "hits" of life on ourselves or they fit into the category of "Life Happens," sometimes the "hits" can really hurt. The "hits" we do not deserve are always the hardest to deal with. Maybe you are dealing with an "I got what I deserved" hit. Whatever the case may be, the Father does not withhold His love depending on whether or not our pain is deserved or undeserved. He wants to be our Comforter in and through *any* painful situation.[1]

Christians Aren't Perfect, Just Forgiven makes a great bumper sticker.[2] However, the reality of my thirty-nine years of ministry experience tells me that a majority of church folks (especially the "churchy-church" people) know this to be true in theory but: (A) believe only certain sins, primarily their own, are *really* forgiven or; (B) although they know better, they really believe Christians should be almost perfect (or at least those in ministry).

As we look back several thousand years removed from the people listed in Hebrews 11's "Hall of Faith" remember, we are completely removed from the headlines, rumors, and gossip that ran rampant during the days following their faux pas. Plus, we can read their lives endings and see how God used them big time, in spite of their flaws. Although we read of how Noah passed out drunk,[3] Abraham was a liar,[4] Jacob a deceiver,[5] and Moses committed murder,[6] we do not have to deal with these scandals! And let us not forget King David, the womanizer who put a contract out on a certain "Hebrew Honey's" husband.[7]

However, that was *then* and we have to live *now* where we could barely tolerate such embarrassments as the "Television Jimmys" of the late '80's. Or if some high profile person of notoriety in our conservative Christian camp says something "off the wall" *stupid*, we are ready to throw them away. "How could they say *that*?!" "How could they do *that*?!" "If they *really* knew the Lord, they would not be doing *that*!" I cannot help but wonder if the "*that*" that is in the lives of people of notoriety does not actually cause the rest of us to come face to face with the "*that*" that is in our own lives and rather than realize and deal with our own hurt, pain, and/or flaws in general, it's much easier to stone those wounded and/or flawed in general and get them out of our sight.

For ten years now, I have pretty much carried myself not so much as a second class saint but more so as an "embarrassed saint." No longer ashamed because Jesus bore my shame[8] and I realized there was no need for both of us to bare it, but still

I was *embarrassed*. I have operated from the mindset that successful people, *especially* those in ministry, don't walk the path of life that I have walked. Combine this with the judgmental mindset of those in the family of God (including of course my "brothers" and "sisters" in the ministry) who walk with a verbal bag of stones, ready to begin on short notice the process of stoning, have, at times, made throwing down the bat and walking off the field look *real* good. Then there are the real "classics" who have *only* heard me on radio, seen me on television, or seen me at a public gathering yet have had a revelation of my heart and have been *divinely* appointed as judge and jury of my life.

So it is truly a "God thing" that through all of the stone throwing, criticisms, and "positive" statements like "you'll drop out of church and be shackin' with someone," the Lord has kept me swinging in the ballgame of life! If you have ever wondered or are currently wondering if you are going to make it in/through (*fill in the blank with your particular situation*), this book is for you. At the risk of sounding trite, if I can keep swinging in the baseball game of life, believing that God *still* has great plans in store, *you* can too! Simply because, if you genuinely know the Lord Jesus, the same Holy Spirit who dwells in me, dwells in you, therefore you too can *Keep Swinging* in the one of a kind ballgame called Your Life![9]

CHAPTER 1

A GREAT START...WHAT HAPPENED?

Principle number 1: Realize WHERE U ran of the baselines
OUTSIDE

My childhood was that of a Beaver Cleaver, type household. Being the youngest of four, with my oldest sibling being seventeen years older, meant that my mom and dad were older and had mellowed. Daddy gave his life to Christ somewhere between seven and eight years before I "discovered America." Some of my earliest and fondest memories are of going to Sunday School and Vacation Bible School. My mother was a stay- at-home mom who was usually home when I returned from school. Mom and Dad were married fifty-nine-and-a-half years until death, Daddy did part. Moving only twice during my childhood, I attended the same school all the way through my senior year in high school. I began in public preaching ministry at the ripe young age of fourteen, and although Daddy did not particularly like preachers, he was generally encouraging.

By nineteen, I had already been on radio, preached in four states, and had two football stadium crusades under my belt. I also had the incredible opportunity of traveling with a couple of "big time" evangelists of that era during the *Jesus Move-*

ment. It was my privilege to be a part of some of the greatest church and city-wide crusades in our nation's history. I even had a great time in the Marine Corps. In Boot Camp, for some reason I was able to realize that it was not anything personal when Drill Instructor Sergeant McCully knocked the wind out of me with only one elbow. He just had a job to do. While stationed with the Third Marine Division, in Okinawa, I had the opportunity to preach the first revival meetings in base chapels in the South Pacific. When I "hit campus" at Howard Payne University, doors quickly opened as I was asked to speak at various campus events, the biggest one being the *Bi-Centennial Homecoming Chapel.*

Recently, I have come to a new dimension of understanding as to what Romans 8:28 is saying. This well known verse is not saying that only specific, challenging instances in our not too distant past are "working together for our good," but rather, since conception, God has strategically engineered and allowed the circumstances of my life, I believe "for such a time as this." However, the truth concerning Romans 8:28 does not contradict Hosea 4:6, which says "My people perish for lack of knowledge." At the risk of sounding like I am playing the "blame game," let me delve into, "what happened."

Although there were many good experiences and lessons during the years of hanging out with the two "big-time" evangelists (henceforth referred to as BTE's) during the era that I mentioned above, they were rebels, with a cause no doubt, but nevertheless rebels, which definitely has its good points, at times. However, during these moldable, impressionable teenage years, they modeled in front of me that it was not that bad to have certain known sin as long as you behaved yourself in public. Then if the right buttons were pushed during the crusade, God would bless. One BTE especially taught by example to buck the system and live on the edge of controversy at all times. The men of whom I speak had not finished college, married in their late teens, and were *huge* successes.

Previously, I mentioned that my parents gave me a great heritage, home, and foundation for my life. BUT, as I had already discovered about the BTE's, my parents were not perfect either. Giving direction and counsel about some of life's most important events was not exactly their strong suit. *Minor* building blocks to success, such as education and who to marry, for some reason were left to the realm of, "he's sharp, he'll make it."

In recent years, I have discovered that this was not uncommon for many of the *Builder Generation*, who had won the war and are truly one of the greatest generations in our nation's history. After much thought and analyzing the situation, my theory is this. The majority of them came from solid, stable homes and when they spoke "...'til death do us part," they *really* meant it. Therefore they never gave a second thought but what their offsprings, the *Baby Boomers*, would live out that commitment as well.

On top of the fact that they had made life so much *easier* for us than it was for them. And with that mindset, should not our marriages be easier as well!

Let me digress for a paragraph or two. Prior to the Second World War, our world was much smaller. For the most part, people married someone from whose family they had grown up around and knew the certain "bent" that particular family had. They were more aware that two people never just married each other, but rather that a marriage is two families coming together. Plus, there was a societal disdain for a person divorcing unless there was a real reason and all attempts at reconciliation had failed.

However, with the onslaught of World War II, "GI Joe" was suddenly thrust in front of women who looked a lot different than the girl next door. Thus, the *"for your eyes only"* age was ushered in with more of the emphasis being on the physical attraction and little regard for a person's background or family heritage. Although, yes, initially the physical is what we see, the truth of "the apple not falling too far from the tree" has never changed, even with our society being all consumed with physical attraction. Sadly, this mindset was dominant even in evangelical youth groups of the '60's and '70's, only they went one step further. Basically the atmosphere was that as long as two people had sex and Jesus in common, what more did they need to make a marriage!?! Is there any question why there is an epidemic of divorce among marriages of 20, 25, and so sadly 30 years? Divorce is rampant between individuals who grew up in the church and came from parents with lasting marriages. Good people who after many years woke up and tragically said, "Other than the children, we don't remotely have anything in common." Hopefully we are learning that there is so much more to being "equally yoked" than just two people who are "born again."

The wonderful mother of our three children and I also came from homes in which both sets of parents had marriages that lasted until one member of the union died. Here is the synopsis. It is not a right or wrong, good or bad. This is just the way it was. My sweet, tender, young bride's parents lived in the same house in which she came home from the hospital to, until they both went home to be with the Lord. Her daddy worked the same job at the Post Office until he retired. They were members of the same Baptist Church with a pastor who never made waves or stood up to deacons.

The mindset in my household, however, was the combination of both of my parent's background of "keep moving on!" and an entrepreneurial spirit that said, "I was looking for a job when I found this one!" Actually, I come from a long line of "bull-heads" and some of the most opinionated people on the face of God's green earth.

Even in this season of my life, after all of the breaking, chastening, and mellowing God has done in my life, I am still a shock to the average person's system. Simply combine everything that I have already told you about myself and rewind the clock by thirty years to a younger man, just out of the Marine Corps, with very few inhibitions, who never met a stranger, and who *knew* that he too would be a BTE and be preaching to the masses by the time he was twenty-five! Oh my gosh, I had to have shocked/scared the stuffing out of that precious young woman! Within three years of marriage, we had moved four times. The fourth move, just a *minor* one to another state in which we were not even real sure "where we were going once we got there?" Mind you those were college days, but nevertheless. Also, I had blown through four jobs by that time. I was going for all of the "gusto" there was to experience out of ministry and life. Although my heart was right, you must understand that most zealots do not even show signs of growing a brain until age forty, at least! When the professor told a class of preacher boys how we needed to just gear ourselves to finish college and go right on through seminary, I remember thinking, "Why do I need to go to seminary? There is a world that is going to hell in a hand basket. I do not have time for that!"

Is the picture beginning to form in your mind? That of a young, extremely tender, reserved, melancholy/phlegmatic, who during her teenage years did not even listen to the rock-n-roll of a generation who thought they were "born to be wild," living under the same roof with this sanguine/choleric who had a preacher/entertainer/musician mix and who liked his music loud might clash, just a *little bit*? When we were having dinner with Tim LaHaye, probably twenty-five years ago, I'll never forget him saying how extreme "opposites attract, then they attack!"

Should we have remained married and worked through our differences?[10] Without a doubt! Did we need help and counsel early on before it was too late? You better know it! (Hey there, you, yeah you! Don't be whispering!) I can hear you saying, "It's never too late as long as two people are still married!" Oh yes, what I have said does not contradict what I have taught for years that in marriage, "there is never a mountain too big to climb with God's help, just people who are either unwilling or too hurt to climb the mountain."[11] This is exactly what happens though when two people beat each other up over a period of years, bloodied and bruised beyond recognition. At that point (anyone who has been through this will back me up), all you can think of is easing the pain (which is stinkin' thinkin' because you have no earthly idea of the real pain of divorce that you will experience, nor of all of the fall-out that comes with the "single again" life).

For those fifty percent of you who have not gone through it (hopefully you never will, believe me, if there is any way to avoid it, please do whatever it takes), divorce is like a hand grenade that explodes in a person's mental, emotional, and spiritual well being. The people who tragically experience this explosion are wounded. They will not be themselves for awhile, and chances are they WILL do something stupid. Whether it is working a hundred hours a week, eating themselves into oblivion, drinking, drugging, the "sexual smorgasbord," dating, or working out in excess, please remember, this is not the big picture of their life!

With all of the events that I have had control over as well as the ones that I have not, the bottom line is: I alone am responsible for the wrong that I have done and the stupid career along with other choices that I have made during my life. Being a "know-it-all," bullhead, zealot has had its consequences. But surely it must break the heart of God that His kids cannot be as honest about their past failures and present struggles as the world is. The fact that we are forgiven should cause us to have the attitude that if Holy God can forgive and accept a person's past and present, therefore we can as well!

Don't Forget:

Realize where U ran outside of the base lines.

CHAPTER 2

IT'S OKAY TO SAY, "I BLEW IT!"

Principle Number 2: Realize that U R not a ROTTEN person because U ran the base lines OUTSIDE

During my all too brief time in my Marine Corps, I was *gung-ho!*

It was a special time in my life that will never again be duplicated. No bills. A work schedule geared to staying in top physical shape. Three square meals a day, none of which did I have to cook or clean up afterwards. My choice of colors as to what to wear each day was pretty much green or green. It was truly a great season in my life.

As mentioned earlier, I was privileged to have preached the first revival meetings on base chapels in the South Pacific. This was due to the vision of Navy Chaplain Andrew Johnson. The first revival meeting took place at the *Sea Bee* base to which this man of God was assigned. Before the first service he introduced me to Marine Colonel C.T. Jones, who "happened" to be my Commanding Officer, whom I had not met at the time. During the course of the service, Col. Jones and I formed a friendship that transcended the normal officer/enlisted relationship. For a "full-bird" colonel to address me by my first name around the base was somewhat unusual but definitely a status symbol. After all of these years, I still think the Mess Sergeant was convinced that I was a "plant" to spy on the mess hall. The last few months of my tour, the guys on the "chow line" seemingly were instructed to give me "seconds" or anything else I wanted. Of course the guys would razz me about the Colonel being "my old buddy."

One night during this "great status symbol" period, I was on "fire watch" in the barracks during the "wee hours." This "highly dangerous" duty consisted of two hours of sitting in a chair, taking a walk through the barracks whenever I wanted, and/or reading a *Mad Magazine* to stay awake. One particular night, for a brief period, I failed at one of the "minor" "fire watch to-do's." Staying awake! And what really made it bad was that I got busted and written up by the Sergeant of the Guard.

There I was, the "Evangelist of Marines" and a friend of the Colonel, *written up!* Article 15! I had made it until nearly the end of my enlistment without being written up. I had to do something! *Aha, since the First Sergeant seemed to like me, I'll schmooze him to schmooze the Sergeant Major, who is in charge of "Office Hours," and get him to schmooze this thing under the rug*, I thought to myself! (As I'm writing this, thirty-one years later, I'm feeling like, *Oh no, I was involved, even back then, in what could have been one of the first evangelists cover up scandals!*)

Wasting no time, I went in to see the First Sergeant as soon as possible. I explained to him how I had an impeccable record and this just would not be a good thing for me, a friend of the Colonel's, to have an Article 15 on MY record. I will never forget the lesson he taught me that day when he looked at me from across his desk and said, "Moore, just take your *(certain part of the anatomy)* chewing like a man. It doesn't mean you're a bad Marine. It just means you screwed up. Learn from it and go on!"

The fact that you may have run outside of the baselines of life, does not make you a bad person. I understand that for some of us, the baselines were made *so unclear* that it was extremely hard to figure out where we were supposed to run. Some of us got pushed out of the lines, while others of us chose to run out. The "why" is nowhere near as important as the "where" we left the baselines. And in the ballgame of life, it is paramount that we realize where we ran out of the baselines and more times than not, we will take a hit. Remember, admitting that you did something wrong does not in and of itself mean that you're a bad person.

In dealing with the "woman caught in adultery," Jesus did not call her a "whore" and grill her as to "why" she did what she did. I am convinced that there was always "the air" about Him in which although He did not *condone* sin, at the same time, He did not *condemn* the sinner. In this particular case, he *commissioned* her by telling her to simply "Go and sin no more."[12]

Any person, over the age of twenty-five, who says they have no regrets is either a liar or a fool! One common thread that the "All Israelis Team" whom I mentioned in the *Introduction* had is that when they "blew it," they all knew what it was to pick them- selves up, wash themselves off with God's forgiveness and go on! Your actions may have really been B-A-D! Always remember, though, Almighty God deemed you worthy enough to send His only begotten Son to die on an old rugged cross in order to forgive your sin nature that caused your bad actions, saving you and giving you a brand new life![13] Since there is "no condemnation to those who are in Christ Jesus,"[14] let us not be afraid to admit that we have willingly done bad things, made poor choices, or just flat put *ourselves* before what we *knew* was the right thing to do.

If you have never really received the forgiveness that Christ paid the price for when He died on the cross, it may be *extremely* hard to forgive yourself. If you have genuinely experienced God's forgiveness and have still "blown it," I do not know about you, but I have become pretty proficient in the art of beating myself up. "How could I have done that!" "But I knew better." And then the one that really justifies self mutilation, "I knew God was telling me not to (*fill in the blank.*")

Although there is no doubt in my mind that I have angered the Lord and yes, I am sad to say that I have also brought reproach on His name, do you know that there is never a time in which our Heavenly Father does not desire fellowship with me, or you? Even as angry as those ever so fickle *Kids of Israel* made Him, there was never a, "Well if you're going to do *that* then get out of my house, and don't come back!"

As a matter of fact, after they had offended Him by saying that they did not want Him to be their king, He said in 1Samuel 12:20 - 22, "...You *have* committed all this evil, yet do not turn aside from following the Lord, but serve the Lord with all your heart. And you must not turn aside, for then you would go after futile things which can not profit or deliver, because they are futile. For the Lord will not abandon His people on account of His great name, because the Lord has been pleased to make you (yeah YOU) a people for Himself." (I added the last parenthesis.)

That was the New American Standard version. The RMRV (Ron Moore Revised Version) says it this way, "Yeah, you've blown it big time, but don't stop coming back to the Lord and serving Him cause then you're really gonna make a mess of things!"

Now then, I must ask, where did you run outside of the baselines in the game of life and/or your Christian walk? At this point, it does not matter why. Is there a desire to keep swinging with the joy, peace, and happiness that you once had? Then agree with God, that where you ran out of the baselines was wrong. This is what 1John 1:9 means when it says, "confess." You may not feel great sorrow at this point but obedience does not always mean that we understand *why* our actions were wrong but rather from the standpoint that whatever God says concerning our thoughts and actions, we are going to agree with Him. If we do agree with Him that what we have done is sin, this verse goes on to say that, "He is faithful and just to forgive us…and to cleanse us from all unrighteousness."

Remember…

U R not a rotten person because U ran out of the baselines, if you have agreed with God, U R 4-GIVEN!

CHAPTER 3

KNOWING WHO YOU ARE

Principle number 3: U R who GOD says U R…

When our children were known as the "wee three," often times I would drive them to school. During the earlier years when they were all under the same school roof, "ol' Dad's" daily "drop-off" ritual usually went something like, "I love you, have a GREAT day and remember who you are!"

Inevitably, one of them would respond while giggling with, "Who are we Daddy?" And my response was usually the same, "You're children of the King,[15] you're the righteousness of God in Christ,[16] you're a joint heir with Jesus!"[17] No, they probably did not understand much of what that meant, but I wanted those facts to go in to their mental recorders. The truth of the statements could be revealed later.

Fast forward the clock by about fifteen years when my marriage to their mother had failed, and I was experiencing what I now affectionately refer to as my "Dark Days of Dallas." One day it became evident that they "got it!" As I was leaving to return to Dallas, knowing that I was living in tough times, one of them said, "Remember who you are Daddy!" Wow! It did soak in! For the next three hours the love of God was so real as I drove south on Interstate 35. Now in order to fully appreciate what I just said, you need to have some insight into those of us who are in vocational ministry. Far too many of us give and give and give God's love without receiving it ourselves. Oh I do not mean we are not born again, but as far as zeroing in on the fact that God *really loves* me, I confess that I do not do that anywhere near as often as I should. When the Hosanna/Integrity singers sang, "I have redeemed you, I have called you by name, child you are mine," on my car's cassette tape player, lights flashed and bells clanged as the truth of God's love for me got into my spirit!

When we begin to see ourselves as our heavenly Father sees us, it will energize not only our season in the game of life, it will catapult us into an entirely new dimension as to how the resurrection of Christ actually applies to our lives! You must understand, Jesus did not conquer death, hell, and the grave in order to just fulfill prophecy. Nor did He come out of the tomb on the third day for a great publicity stunt that would be talked about two thousand years later. One of the *main reasons* that He arose to sit at the right hand of the Father was to enable us with the ability of not swinging at the curve balls of Satan, sin, and self that are thrown at us in this life.[18]

Thinking of ourselves as God's children whose position "in Christ"[19] is that of righteous and "complete in Him"[20] is not being cocky or arrogant! Of course we all have faults and sin willingly on a regular basis! However, in Romans 8:33 & 34, the question is asked, "Who will bring a charge against (or accuse) God's elect? God is the one who justifies: who is the one who condemns? Christ Jesus is He who died, yes, rather who was raised, who is at the right hand of God who also intercedes *for* us."

No one likes to have their children "ragged on." To this day, if you were to stop me on the street and begin wailing about the faults of my children and telling me that they are no good, I will cut you off before you have the opportunity to go very far! Is it because I am ignorant of their faults? I think not! But number one, they are not *your* children, and number two, the paint is still wet on the canvas of their lives. The last chapter of their lives has by *no means* been written.

Hello! What about our heavenly Father? Do you think He appreciates or takes it lightly when we think of and/or speak of ourselves as second class, 'ner-do-well saints? Although He knows *all* of our faults, warts, blemishes, and basically the areas in which we still have an enormous room for growth in, He says that we are "justified,"[21] and He is making "intercession *for* us."[22] After graduating from a Christian University with advanced studies in Bible and attending a theologically conservative seminary (Okay I confess, I am a Masters Degree dropout. Whoa, do I feel better), the best definition that I have heard of the term "justified" is "just-as-if-I'd never sinned." That my friend is a Wow! If we have accepted the new birth into our lives, Almighty God looks at us as if we had never sinned.

And did you notice that it does not say that He is making intercession critical of nor condemning of us? Did you catch that? He is making intercession for us. Do you know that God is for you, not against you? In fact, He is absolutely committed to making everything that was real in the life of Jesus real in your life,[23] which will not happen quickly or instantly. Our

Daddy (Romans 8:15 "Abba Father" simply means "Daddy") has never looked at us, even while we were in the middle of our nastiest thoughts, ugliest deeds, or when our most fowl and vile words were being spoken, and said, "I can't bee-lieve I saved them! I wish that I had never let them into my kingdom!" That memo has never been sent from Headquarters Universe. The writer of Hebrews tells us that our great high priest, the Lord Jesus Christ, understands and identifies with our faults and weaknesses.[24]

As long as we continue to see ourselves as good for nothing, low-down, scum-of-the-earth sinners in which "If we're saved, we're barely saved," we will not experience resurrection power. Each time life throws us a curve ball, we will continue to swing and miss. You may have grown up in a church as I did, or you may be apart of one now, in which there is something seemingly spiritual about tearing yourself down and beating yourself up.

In all actuality, there is *nothing* spiritual about it because you are talking about one of God's kids, whom He loves dearly and He does not appreciate it! Therefore, since He declares that we are "the righteousness of God in Christ," "justified," and that we are His children of whom He is not ashamed to be called our Father,[25] who has plans of good and not harm for our lives[26], do you not think it is time we start thinking and speaking of ourselves as God does?

Within the first few minutes of standing on the yellow footprints at the Marine Corps Recruit Depot in San Diego, we were told in a tone of voice we could understand that, "You are now in the United States Marine Corps! You are the President's own! You are a part of *the* elite fighting force of these United States! You and your rifle are a majority! You will walk like a Marine, talk like a Marine and conduct yourself at all times as a United States Marine! You are now part of the proud, the few, and the brave!"

After month upon month of having that drilled into your head, you actually begin to believe that "you da baddest thing that ever stepped out." This is exactly why we hear of the Marine Corps glory stories in which twenty five men in a rifle platoon held 2,000 Japanese at bay for days at a time during the Second World War. Not because every Marine stands 6'5", weighs 250 pounds and eats nails for breakfast. Simply because *they know who they are!* They are the President's own, the elite fighting force, and the combination of them and their rifle make a majority!

When we get it in our spirits who we are IN Christ and that we and Jesus make a majority, watch out hell because nothing will stop a child of the King from playing all "nine innings" in this game of life!

Realize

Your *ACTIONS* do not change who U R! And that THE TRUEST thing about U is NOT what U think, hear, feel, or C but what God's Word says about U! The goal is for our actions to MATCH UP with who God says that we R!

CHAPTER 4

LET THE COACH BE THE COACH

Principle number 4: U Do YOUR job and Let God Do His

One of the many great joys of parenting was practicing as well as coaching little league baseball and softball teams when the children were small. At the risk of sounding old, it does seem just the other day when my son David got his first hit, ran to first base, and turned around with a frantic look that screamed, "What do I do next!" I guess "Coach Daddy" had forgotten to teach him that when you get a hit, you are supposed to keep running and try to make it to as many bases as possible, *especially* when the first base coach is yelling, "Go, Go!"

One team that stands out during my days of coaching had a particular member we affectionately referred to as "Jumpin' Jimmy." When we first began practicing for the season, "Jumpin'" had basically never been made to do anything that he did not want to do. If I said, "Throw the ball," he wanted to hold on to the ball. If I said, "Run," he wanted to stay where he was. Much to this coach's dismay, not only did "Jumpin' Jimmy" always think that he had a better idea, he was usually quite vocal about it as well.

During one fateful practice when I could "take no mo'" Jimmy and I had a "heart to heart." In no uncertain terms I "informed him" that if he was going to continue on that team, he was going to play ball how I wanted him to, when I wanted him to, and where I wanted him to, or he was not going to play at all! Because that young boy knew that I loved him and cared about him, I want you to know he made a 180 degree turn around. Not only did he let me be the coach, my older daughter Jennifer, who had been in his class the year before and then again in the school year following that baseball season, said he was a totally different "Jumpin' Jimmy" in class as well.

What a difference it makes when we allow the God of the Universe to also be the Head Coach of our lives. I fear that far too many of we who are on the team, like the Pharisees of ancient times, have added our own set of rules and regulations as to how we are supposed to play the game. With the "big sin/little sin" theology continuing to be espoused in Sunday School classes and from pulpits around America, we have portrayed the Christian life as much more *complicated* and for the most part BOR-ING! These are two adjectives that God *never* intended to be used in conjunction with the Christian life. Have you ever noticed how, amongst people with this mindset, feel "their sin" is never quite as bad as "your sin?" I am so thankful that Jesus died for sin, period!

God says that there is, "no condemnation to those who are in Christ Jesus,"[27] and in another passage the Apostle Paul goes on to write, "...forgetting what's behind, and reaching forward to what lies ahead, I press on toward the goal..."[28] And finally, from the angle of athletic competition, he writes about running "the race with the aim to win."[29] After all of these years, I think I am finally starting to get it! Our primary focus is not to be on whether or not we are doing everything right. Nor should it be on trying to be "holy," which for so many Christians means trying to act or look a certain way and talk with a certain Christian-*eaze*. How many evangelical church members think "God is smiling on them" because they try so hard not to "cuss, smoke, drink, or spit in the sink," and by all means, at all costs, abstain from d-d-dancing?!?

When we try to play Holy Spirit in our own or anyone else's life, we will always overlook the areas that God says are important. The picture I am getting is that our primary focus is to live the life that God has called us to live.[30] Then, striving at all times to be in the process of becoming what He has called us to be[31] and as a result of those two functions, doing what He has called us to do. As we experience these three, "living, becoming, and doing," we can count on the enemy, who wants to "steal, kill, and destroy,"[32] coming against us. The late, great Babe Ruth was not known as the "Homerun King" because every time he swung his bat, he hit a homerun. He was also known as the "Strikeout King!" Just because the "churchy church" people never get "called out" does not necessarily mean they are following the Coach's game plan for their life.

Between the world, the flesh, and the devil,[33] there will be numerous times in which we strike out, miss the balls that are thrown our way, and just flat drop the fly ball out of our glove as we play in this baseball game of life! But fasten your seat belt! When God saved us He knew that there would be those times of fatigue in which we slip into the "me, Me, ME" syndrome. And then the times in which one of life's "surprise balls out of left field" comes at us hard and fast, without time to really think the situation through, and we do or say something stupid that we definitely regret! He even knew about the times that we would flat out know that what we were about to do was wrong, it was sin, but we did it anyway! Yet He still saved us, forgave us, and called us His own.[34]

Personally, I have spent far too much time being knocked down on the playing field of life, wallowing in guilt and shame. Without a doubt, I have spent too much time beating myself up with, "I can't believe I did that. How could I do _____ _____!" (Don't forget to fill in the blank with the particular instance, and/or many instances as is the case with me, in which you swung at a ball, knowing it was not in the strike zone.) Although we spend far too much time staying knocked down on the playing field due to "mess ups" and our own imperfections, life continues to go by way too fast and a lost world is dying and spending eternity separated from the God who loves them.

If an earthly coach knows when to take a player out of a game that will be forgotten in fifty years, do we not think that our Heavenly Coach knows when to send us to the dugout? Whether or not we need a serious "heart to heart" during the "seventh inning stretch" or, yes, even when to take us out of the game? Mind you, what we do in this game of life will be remembered fifty thousand years from now. In other words, let the coach be the coach! Our job is to play the game of life that He has called us to play. When we do not play according to His rules, He knows how, when, and where to correct us. He deals with us as His "children" because He is our Father, who loves us unconditionally and always wants what is best for us.[35]

Does this mean that we do not deal with issues, faults, or sins? Not at all![36] What I am saying is that we do not have the time nor are we called to do what the Coach has committed Himself to do. The verses following the much talked about and often quoted verse, at least in this book, Romans 8:28, go on to tell us why "all things" are working together for our good. It is not just so that we can be a happier, better person with a higher self esteem. The fact is, Romans 8:29 tells us the reason that "all things" are working together for our good is in order to conform us to his image! And let me go one step farther, at the risk of putting you on overload: The Lord is not primarily concerned with our happiness! But He is, however, desperately concerned with our holiness![37] Here is *yet another nugget* of good news! As we allow Him to work His work of holiness in our lives, we will be happy! I have heard it said many times that, "God will make us holy if He has to drag us kicking and screaming." I, however, know without a doubt that the only way that He makes any of us holy is by dragging us kicking and screaming! Why is this you ask? (Isn't it amazing how I can hear what you're thinking?) "Elementary my dear Watson," because our flesh does not want to die! Learning to die to self is a slow and painful process.[38]

Does it not just make sense that if Christ "learned discipline through the things He suffered,"[39] plus the truth of the statement He made to "da' boys" that if He did not die, He would not be glorified,[40] there is *no way* that we will go up to the next level with God without suffering? Who do we think we are? Do we think we are better than the Lord Jesus Himself, thinking that we can learn to take up our cross and follow Him without suffering? Should we seek suffering? Are you crazy?! I always wonder about people who "pray" to be broken. Believe me, if we will concentrate on playing the particular position in this game of life that He has called us to, our Heavenly Coach knows "how" and "when" to send us running laps around the field until we give up and decide to do life His way. He sent the "Kids of Israel" taking laps around Mount Sinai.[41] Little did I know those years ago that I was signing up to be part of the "Mileage Plus" plan for the number of laps that I would eventually take around Mount Sinai! I can truly say, however, the joy has been and still is in daily playing the game. Yes, I have been struck out, tagged out, and thrown out many times, but our Heavenly Coach has always been faithful to perform what is best for this player. Although I am still learning how to swing, pitch, catch, and field the ball, He has brought me a long way from when I first walked onto the field.

If you will simply determine that no matter what kind or how many curve balls of life you are thrown, you are going to stay in the game and "little by little"[42] become who and what He has called you to be, then all of Heaven will back up your decision so that even when you are hit with the ball or sent to the dug out for awhile, you will know that it is just a matter of time until you are back in the game. The Coach did not choose you for the team just to leave you on the bench. There are no permanent bench warmers on God's team!

ALLOW the *COACH* 2-B the *COACH*

U play the game!

CHAPTER 5

Overcoming Stinkin Thinkin

Principle number 5: Think of yourself as the homerun hitter U R becoming!

The Green Mountain Baseball Association of Lakewood, Colorado, did not do T-Ball. Coach pitch was the way to teach young athletes how to properly swing the bat. Also, there was no "win/loss" record for the little guys, but we had bundles of fun. However, as the Head Coach, I felt like those young "boys of summer" needed an ego boost. Prior to the games, on the far other side of the park, with the same fervor of a tent revivalist, I would get the team into a frenzy as I would scream, "Who's the number one team in Green Mountain?" And away we would trot onto the field yelling in unison, "We're number one! We're number one!" I just had this "gut feeling" that if those precious young boys thought of themselves as the Number 1 team, they would play like a Number 1 team plays.

At the risk of sounding like a "positive thinking guru," let me ask you, what do you "think" about yourself? Let me "preface" the Biblical principle that I am about to espouse with a couple of thoughts: first, a Bible principle will[43] work in this life for people who are not and have no plans of receiving the "new birth." I.E., if you put others first, that action will come back to bless you. If a man loves his wife and treats her like a queen, in most cases, that woman will treat him like a king. This *alone* is why there is power in positive thinking. God Himself is the quintessential positive thinker. But even if a person's picture is out by the definition of "Optimist" and dies without Christ, can we say eternity is at least *somewhat* longer than even one hundred years of positive thinking in this life?[44] Secondly, the real reason that we who have been born again can think positively (we talked about this in chapter 3) is because of who we are in Christ.

Let me ask you the same question again in this manner. Do you think of yourself as "more than a conqueror?"[45] (Don't start with me! I know what you're thinking!) "But Ron, you don't know about how I allow myself to daydream about romantic nights," or "Ron, I embarrassed myself the way I drooled over that woman with the big chest at the grocery store the other day." Need I say more?

When the enemy kicks our spiritual rears between our shoulders it does tend to plant the seed of *Stinkin' Thinkin'*.[46] Then he waters that seed by laughing at us with, "BOY, a saint you ain't!" And the moment we agree with a, "Gee, I guess I'm not very spiritual at all! Maybe I have never *really* been born again," that is the split second the devil gets a foot in the door of our minds and *Stinkin' Thinkin'* has the opportunity to run wild![47]

POP QUIZ: When we have those kinds of thoughts, can we be used by the Father to show His love to someone who desperately needs to know it? TRUE / FALSE

Obviously the answer is false! This is the bottom line reason that Satan wants to trip us up, because if we are walking by faith, thinking our Father's thoughts about us, then we will do damage to the kingdom of darkness! As long as we think of ourselves as a weakling, "wienie-boy" Christian, that is exactly how we are going to live. Jesus said it this way, "As a man thinks in his heart, so he is." If we will begin to think of ourselves as God thinks of us *before* we are thrown the "curve ball that so easily strikes us out," (Hebrews 12:1 RMRV) there CAN be a "wait a minute, I am walking in the Spirit, with power over the enemy of lust, wandering thoughts, critical spirit, gossipy mouth, internet pornography, _____, or _____, so I do not have to swing at this curve ball." (Once again, fill in the blank with the particular curve ball that you have swung at in the past.) It is not God who is whispering in your ear, "but if that's true, why dost thou getteth thy reareth kicked *so easilyth* in those areas?" We have already established that "the whole truth and nothing but the truth" about you is what God says.

POP QUIZ #2: When our Father chose us to be His kids, He probably thought we would have "it all together." That's why He made the statement about US that we are "more than conquerors." **TRUE / FALSE**

Another obvious! That truth in Romans 8 was written to people like you and me, people who had a plethora of struggles. The fact that we struggle does not change the fact that as believers, we have Holy Spirit Power. Another great word picture of the Christian life is that of a wrestling match.[48] Have you ever seen a real wrestling match in high school, college, or maybe the Olympics? If you have, then you know that there has never been a champion wrestler who has not at times had his opponent on top of him. Yet ultimately the champion wrestler will end the match on top of his opponent!

So stop thinking of yourself as the kid in the kingdom with the big "L" on your forehead. Although your opponent may have been on top of you for days, weeks, months or even years, there is no time like the present to recognize the *Stinkin' Thinkin'* that has cheated you out of the joy of the journey of life! Second Corinthians 10 is another passage about the "combat zone" that we as believers live in. In verse 5, the Apostle Paul writes about destroying thoughts that go against the knowledge of God. No doubt it is easy to accept thoughts like "but my family has been like this for years," "I can't seem to break this habit," "this is just me," and then there are the real kickers of "I've been this way too long," and "how many times have I tried." Whatever Stinkin' Thinkin' thought it might be that acts as your excuse to not walk under the Lordship of Christ, experiencing Holy Spirit power, it does *not* line up with the knowledge of the God of the Bible.

"*Who's your daddy?*" The one and only all powerful, all knowing God of the universe Who asks you the question, "Is there *anything* too hard for me,"[49] that's Who! Years ago, a dear friend of mine was "talkin' trash" about her husband to her pastor's wife. She told of how bad their marriage was and how there was just no hope. Her pastor's wife, another longtime friend of mine, looked across the table and said, "You know I think you're right. Your situation is harder than the resurrection!" When my friend put that in perspective she realized that her marriage problems were not too hard for God! She and her husband are not only happily married for thirty years now, but also have a national marriage seminar and counseling ministry. Therefore I ask, is your moral struggle, financial or marriage problem, health crisis, or kid's driving you crazy problem bigger than the challenge that raising Christ from the dead was for the Father?

Jesus said, "According to your faith, that is what you are going to have."[50] This is a Bible principle seen from Genesis to Revelation. Later on in the New Testament, it is written that, "without faith, it is impossible to please God."[51] That is what I was alluding to a few paragraphs ago when I wrote about the bottom line reason that the enemy wants to trip us up. Simply put, it is a physical and spiritual impossibility to live as a schlock towards God and believe Him to do great deeds in, through, and for your life.

If you reported to your job fifteen minutes late every day, took fifteen of a ten minute break, clocked out fifteen minutes early every day, and took ten minute coffee breaks that lasted twenty minutes, do you think you could march in to the boss's office and ask for a raise with faith that your request would be granted? Probably not! This is why it is so important that we think what our Father thinks about us in order to live as He has told us to live. If we are flagrantly walking in known disobedience, we will not walk by faith allowing Him to do those "great and mighty" things that we have never even thought about.[52]

Does this sound inviting? Experiencing those great and mighty deeds that you have not even thought about? If it does, it does not matter what your past has been! Dare to dig into God's Word and discover what His thoughts are about you. You will not find an example where one of His kids, who is striving to become what He called them to be, "blows it big time" to which He responds, "Well you have really messed up this time. I think you just need to hang it up,'cause it's all over for you!"

That is the difference between King number one and King number two of Israel, Saul and David. Saul, whom God changed his mind about, ceased repenting and began justifying his actions.[53] David however, when confronted even after numerous times of "blowing it," had the overall attitude of, "Lord, I sinned against you and you alone!"[54] This is why he is still known to this day as "a man after God's own heart."

I *dare you* to take responsibility for the times you swung at a ball that you knew you should not have and begin to think the thoughts that God says are "thoughts of welfare and not calamity to give you a future and a hope."[55] (KJV mixed with NASB) When you stop with the *Stinkin' Thinkin'* that goes against the knowledge of God which is only found in His Word, your batting average will "strikingly" improve and you will not be able to give up on whatever it is that you know God wants you to be or do!

R U Thinkin' God's Thoughts About U
OR R U STINKIN' THINKIN'

CHAPTER 6

God's Word: The No Carb Power Bar

Principle Number 6: God's Word is for the Spiritual U what Food is for the Physical U

For a number of years now, athletes and advertisers have known how important nutrition is for those who compete in sporting events. "Wheaties, The Breakfast of Champions" was heralded on the airwaves for many years. With so many people nowadays skipping breakfast, the trend is for the quick and easy. "Don't have time for a bowl of cereal? We've got a bowl of cereal in a bar!" A bowl of cereal shaped like a small candy bar!?! (Give me a break!) But never fear! If you are one of the millions of Americans on overload, time wise, you can also catch a low carb/no carb power bar or power drink for lunch! The bottom line is that over the last thirty years, we as a nation have begun to realize how important good nutrition is for our health.

A few weeks ago I was at the house of the friend in Grapevine, Texas, to whom this book is dedicated. He and his wonderful wife and family of *four* boys were talking about a new power drink with no carbs that they had just discovered. I suppose it was due to my reputation as being somewhat "high energy" and/or hyper that one of their sons, Michael J., spouted off in a bodacious tone of voice, "Don't give Ron one of those! He *definitely* doesn't need one!"

I wish that there was a spiritual power boost bar that I could recommend. Maybe its name would be "spirit boost." I can hear the commercial now, "Don't have time for a quiet time, grab a spirit boost bar on your way to work. You'll get the recommended daily dose of the Holy Ghost as you eat the only candy bar with nuts imprinted with Old Testament as well as New Testament power verses, plus the added benefits from the *only* bar that's been dunked in water imported from the Jordan River!" Would that not be a hoot if there were a product like this!

Fortunately, God in His wisdom knew how desperately we needed to slowly digest the nourishment that only comes from a full complete concentration on His Word. "Slowly digest." While I am not against methods such as "Read the Bible through in '02" in challenging us to read the Bible, however the spiritual nourishment that we desperately need does not come from quantity but from quality. Bible reading is not a matter of "a chapter a day to keep the devil away," but rather realizing the Word of God is to your spirit person what food is for the physical person, i.e., strength![56]

Every serious baseball player knows the importance of good nutrition. As much as I still love the New York Yankees, (or at least the Yankees of the Mickey Mantle/Roger Maris era,) there is no way they could run and hit the ball with great strength and energy if they had not had anything to eat in two weeks. Yet how many of us go for weeks at a time without sitting down for a "home cooked meal of the Word" that the Lord has prepared for us at His table? Certainly God can and does speak to us through Christian radio and television. However, there is no substitute in the midst of our busy schedules for prioritizing time to sit down with the mindset of "Lord, I am here at this place to sit at Your feet and listen to what You have to say to me through Your Word."

As a Marine, I was taught to dress for battle. There is a reason for putting on your helmet, flack-jacket, and combat boots. One of my Drill Instructors (I'm telling you Sgt. McCully could knock the wind out of me with one blow from his elbow) said it so eloquently, "You don't go out ditty-boppin through the jungle with cut-offs and a t-shirt! If you do, you can just count on catching the shrapnel from the enemy."

The bottom line reason that we as believers experience defeat is because most of us are out ditty-boppin' through the jungle of life without being dressed for battle. *Of course* we are going to catch the shrapnel of the enemy when we embark on whatever jungle it is that we spend eight, ten, or twelve hours a day in, if we go there without love, faith, truth, and the sword of the Spirit surrounding our very being.[57]

It will be amazing what will happen when you genuinely spend time alone with Jesus, three, four, five, six, or dare we say *seven* times a week!?! I challenge you, if you do not already, begin to think of God's Word as the absolute spiritual nourishment for your spirit being. Realize that without it, of course Satan will be able to strike you out at the plate on a regular basis.[58]

While the Yankees could not play a decent game of baseball if they had not had anything to eat for two weeks, they also would not win if they only read the game book of baseball that says, "This is the way to play the game." I fear that the flip side of the coin for many of us who have been in church, claiming to have walked with God for years, is that while we may have a detailed knowledge of His Word, doing what the Word tells us to do is another subject.[59] Although the preceding paragraphs are true, yet herein is the reason that the average person on the street has the mindset of, "What difference does it make," concerning the church of the 21st Century.

When they, as well as our children, see that divorce, financial indebtedness, and immorality are virtually the same in the church as it is out of the church, what else are they going to think? This boils down to one huge challenge. Getting the people of the book to do what the book says to do! No doubt, this breaks the heart of God. About eleven years ago when we returned to the "Bible Belt" as a family, I was excited that our children would be living in an area where Jesus was "high profile." Whether it is the ichthus fish on many businesses, the weatherman on Saturday nights saying, "for your drive to church in the morning," or the car lots and pizza places that boldly have scriptures on their electronic signs, Jesus is definitely high profile! I am not complaining mind you. However, it was not too long after we returned that one of the kids said, "Gee Dad, while everyone here goes to Sunday School and Youth Group on Wednesday nights, on Friday and Saturday nights they are out drinking and messing around like everyone else. At least in Colorado the kids who came were serious about wanting to walk with God."

If your "batting average" with the Lord has not been so hot lately, dare to either stay at home or go out and do even just one something that you know He has told you to do.[60] Talk about a boost to our game! Even if it is something that we or our friends consider small, be a *Nike* kind of Christian and "Just do it!" Whether it is loving our spouse, speaking words that build up instead of tear down, taking food to someone who is going through a tough time financially, deleting certain internet sites that you know are not of God, or abstaining from a trip to the water cooler when "Miss Flirty Goodbody" *happens* to be going there or asking "Mr. Holy Hunk" to "lay hands" on you and pray over you after Wednesday night church (no doubt you get transformed, into one of the Beach Boys because you are suddenly "pickin' up good vibrations") just say, "yes" and obey the signals of Jesus, the Head Coach of your day, and you will be *amazed* at the fresh zest you will have for this game of life. Victory produces victory. Even a hit that puts you on first base beats a strike out and will give you fresh excitement to become what He has called you to be, a homerun hitter!

Your SWING at the "home plate" of life will
get STRONGER as U OINK-OUT on &
DO what God's Word tells U to DO

CHAPTER 7

GOD'S ROSIN BAG...FORGIVENESS

Principle Number 7: Get a GRIP & LET GO. U can't change what's happened

Summers were always fun as a young boy. Each summer, beginning in the summer of my ninth birthday, I spent two weeks "working" at my Uncle Alvin's gas station and Dairy Dream Drive-In, in Apache (Mayberry), Oklahoma. The next five years was a steady gig and one of my first entertainment venues where, for a couple of dollars worth of gasoline, I would also clean the windshield, check the oil and air your tires, as well as sing a rousing rendition at the top of my lungs of Roger Miller's "Dang Me," all while I was "takin' care of business."

Then there were usually two weeks at our cabin on Lake Tenkiller, in northeastern Oklahoma. My daddy would take me fishing and skiing every day! Having been in the water for hours at a time, it was amazing, I did not need a *real* bath! Or at least I was able to "con" my mom into believing that I was clean enough. Throughout the summers one thing was always consistent, "Da' Boys of Summer." I would sit and watch baseball games with my daddy most every weekend.

Listening to colorful commentators such as PeeWee Reese and Dizzy Dean and watching the New York Yankees, with Mickey Mantle (who I had the privilege of meeting before he passed away, at a restaurant in Dallas, Texas) and Roger Maris are cherished memories.

Watching the great pitchers of the day reach down and pick up the rosin bag always intrigued me. The way they would stop and pick up that dirty little bag that emitted "white stuff" and roll it around in their hands, all for the *sole purpose* of having the best grip on the ball they could possibly have, simply fascinated me. If all adulthood could be as simple and uncomplicated as my childhood summers, having a grip on life at all times through every season would not be problem. But "life happens," does it not?!? Hurts and bruises are part of the happenings of life, of which if we are not careful, it is so easy to loose the grip that we *think* we have as we go through the "seventh inning stretch" of our lives.

When we swing at the curve balls of life or maybe even step in front of them and get knocked down, what do we do? How do we regain our grip and keep a youthful zest and zeal for the game of life? I am convinced that God has given us a "rosin bag" that will allow us to maintain, regain, or maybe just get a grip on life. This "rosin bag" is none other than forgiveness!

Ahhh! I'm hearing voices again! And you are absolutely right! I do not know how deeply he, she, or "they" hurt you, or what it has cost you. But I do realize that just maybe as you read this book, you feel as though you are not ready to forgive and in the words of the great 21st Century "Country" theologian, Terri Clark, you "just want to be mad for awhile!"

But let me quickly explain what forgiveness is not:
- It's not a feeling,
- It's not condoning what that person has done to you,
- It does not mean that you set yourself up to get hurt again,
- It does not mean the person who hurt you does not have to suffer the consequences.

In the letter to the Ephesians, the old Apostle writes that we are to "forgive others just as Christ forgave us."[61] Christ told us if we did not forgive, we would be turned over to the torturers.[62] Personally, I am NOT into torture! I do admit that keeping short accounts is partially selfish. Repeat, I *do not* like to be tortured! But the simple fact of the matter is that when we (and here comes the "O" word that so few of us in the "no rules and nothing is sacred" society we live in) obey what God tells us, we have a grip on life that cannot be loosened.

Discipleship 101 states that the Father will never ask us to do anything that He has not already given us the power to do. We do not have to wait until the feeling hits us in order to forgive. Like almost every other situation in life, forgiveness is a choice! Since God has already given us the power to do what He has told us to do, we can make the choice to forgive. The practical side of "forgiving as Christ has forgiven us" is to stop and think of all that He has forgiven us of. *(I feel another wow coming on!)* Wow! (I'm afraid I would have popped if I hadn't said that!) I know first hand because of all the times that I have been bathed and cleansed and bathed and cleansed and bathed and cleansed over and over all for the same sin, not to mention all of the others that He has forgiven me of, is forgiving me of, and shall continue to forgive me of! Mind you, I am not speaking of sin that can just be written off as "mistakes." Is sin a mistake? Absolutely! However, I fear that far too often we flippantly refer to "sin" as just a "mistake." However a mistake is like missing your exit while talking on your cell phone or letting the prime rib cook too long in the oven. The offenses against His holiness, both calculated as well as those we spontaneously commit, are far too wrong to just write off as a "mistake." Yet He has forgiven me of it all! That's why when I think of all the outright sin that He has forgiven me of, I can "forgive those who have trespassed against me," to repeat a line of the Model Prayer.[63]

You can forgive those who have hurt you as well. Just remember what all you have been forgiven of and you too can make the choice to forgive. When we make this choice, we may or may not feel like a huge weight has been lifted off of our shoulders. Initially there is normally a tremendous feeling of release, depending of course on the depth of the offense. And depending on the seriousness of the offense, we will more than likely have to continue to make the choice. As I said in essence a few paragraphs ago, we are forgiven, we are being forgiven, and we shall continue to be forgiven, *if* we have genuinely received the work that Christ did on the cross as our *only* claim to salvation and righteousness.[64] That is why after the initial choice to forgive, we may need to do it daily, twice or thrice daily or maybe even hourly for a period of time. The principle is not only that of obedience to God's Word, but of personal freedom as well. Most people do not realize that unforgiveness does not hurt the person toward whom it is directed. It hurts US! The torturers of whom Jesus spoke of are not in the "sweet by and by." The torture of unforgiveness will hurt us in the "nasty here and now." When unresolved anger turns to bitterness, ultimately turning to hatred, it results in a "torture" in this life.[65] Call me selfish if you must, but I want to be free! And who wants to be around someone who is angry, bitter and hates people?

As we continue to forgive, God's hands are free to heal and turn our scabs into scars. A scab can easily be picked off but over a period of time, as we forgive and let God heal, the scab that signified a definite hurt will be turned into a scar that will signify what the Father has brought us through. The scars on the hands and feet of Jesus stand for what He had to go through in order to experience resurrection power. That concept is true in our lives as well. When you stop to think that if Jesus had to suffer in order to go up to the next level, then let me ask again, who do we think that we are that we will not have to suffer in order to have a deeper walk with God. No one enjoys tough times, but in the words of Dr. Robert Schuller, "tough times don't last, tough people do." Choosing to pick up God's rosin bag of forgiveness can sometimes be tough, but remember all that He has forgiven you of and look at the alternative. (Have you ever been around a bitter old person?)

Over twenty years ago, the little church that we had started in the Denver area was shaken by the heinous sin of adultery that I committed while holding the position of pastor. Although I forsook and confessed sin privately to my wife and family and publicly to our church (believe it or not, people were actually set free that night to confess the moral sin that they had kept in their own closet), we still had nearly a complete turnover in membership during the following twelve months. While I believe that most of them forgave me as a brother, they could no longer allow me to be their pastor and I understand that.

During the next year and a half while my wife and I were in counseling, our local church was healing as well. One of the people God used to accomplish this was our Associate Pastor. I will call him "Tim." Tim was experienced in ministry, seemingly mature in the Lord and I counted us blessed to have him. His wife, whom I will call "Ursula," was the best piano player we had during that four year pastorate. However, little did I know of another great theological truth that was espoused by the '70's Motown group, Undisputed Truth, when they sang, "…smilin' faces, smilin' faces sometimes, they don't tell the truth! Can you dig it?" (Go ahead, sing along.) Little did I know how he was undermining our ministry just when we thought we had gotten on our feet again as a church. Although we were regularly seeing people receive the gift of salvation, marriages strengthened, lives touched, and bodies healed, because of innuendos spoken by Tim to the flock such as, "I'm hungry for a *real* move of the Holy Spirit," doubt was cast on the validity of our ministry. The search that was led by good old Bro. Tim and Ursula for spiritual exhibitionism was on. "Spiritual exhibitionism" is the belief that you have not really met with God unless pews are being jumped, chandeliers are being swung from, and at least five people are foaming at the mouth! On top of casting doubt as to the spirituality of our ministry, Bro. Tim was putting out the word that I had been hitting on his wife! His own father-in-law, in a conversation several weeks after the fact, told me of how he had started talking this trash to him. However, being the wise, old man of God that he was and knowing Tim the way he did, his response was, "Well then if there's sin in the camp, let's go right now and confront Pastor Ron about this matter." Pastor Dave said it was almost comical how fast Tim began "crawdadin' it!"

So with only three weeks until Christmas that year, Tim and Ursula split our church in order to start their own, taking not only members but about $800.00 per month in revenue. Granted, $800.00 is not much to a larger church, but for our congregation who on a good Sunday struggled to reach one hundred and twenty-five in attendance, that was a *lot* of money.

And to add insult to injury, Tim and Ursula not only started their own church, they started it diagonally across the street from ours, literally a baseball's throw away. Every Sunday, as I would have to drive by and think about the hurt and hardship they caused us, it ate my lunch! Finally, after several months of getting bent out of shape every time I drove by, I made the choice to practice what I had preached about forgiveness to so many others. I got tired of driving by their church and having to confess sin as I drove up to our church. On that particular, fateful day, when I said, "Lord, I want to line up with Your Word and make the choice to forgive Tim, Ursula, and those who went with them, bless them, they really did not know of what they were doing," a load was lifted! From that Sunday on I would drive by and pray, "Bless them, Lord. I choose to forgive them." Did they thrive? No, they actually paid a dear price for their deeds.

If you are struggling with hurts of the past you can be healed. You do not have to wait for a special zap from heaven. If you have genuinely experienced the "new birth" in Christ, you have the power to make the choice to forgive and let the healing begin! I promise you, by picking up God's rosin bag of forgiveness, you will again be able to get a grip on the life that He has for you.

THINK of how MUCH God has 4-GIVEN U and it's MUCH easier to build a BRIDGE and GET OVER IT!

CHAPTER 8

BENCHED AND BROKEN

Principle Number 8: 2-Whom MUCH Is Given MUCH Is Expected

Pete Rose, now there was a guy who knows what it is to keep swinging. After his first eleven times at bat for the major leagues his record was a consistent, no hits. However, possessing a "never say die" attitude, when he stepped up to the plate for his twelfth try, little did he know the swing that made contact with the ball that day would only be the first of 4,256 career hits. Although it has been twenty years since his last time at bat, this record has yet to be broken. With Rookie of the Year, Most Valuable Player, and World Series MVP honors, three World Series rings, and a twenty-five year Major League career which included getting up to bat 14,053 times, to say that Pete Rose is truly a baseball great is truly an understatement. But he was a gambler.

Heroic people tend to have heroic flaws. As I wrote the above paragraph, it reminded me of how our accomplishments do not go unnoticed either. God does remember what we have accomplished. In Second Kings 5, He talks about the accomplishments of Naaman, who was a captain of the army, which in our day would be equal to a General. It says that he was "highly respected" and that because of his skill, the Lord brought about a great victory. And saving the best for last, at least in the opinion of this Marine, the scripture says that he was a "valiant warrior." The cry of my heart is to be known as a valiant warrior in God's 21st Century Marine Corps. But again, after all of these accolades, "valiant warrior," is followed up with, "But he was a leper." Granted, Naaman did not choose to be a leper. But remember, pain is pain whether deserved or not. None of Naaman's past accomplishments could stop the pain of leprosy. Neither will all of Pete Rose's great accomplishments in the game of baseball stop the pain in his heart over what seems to be an irreversible fact that he will never be inducted into the Baseball Hall of Fame, due to gambling on Major League baseball games. And not just the other team's games, by his own admission, he gambled on his own beloved Cincinnati Reds where he had become the manager. The character challenge both Naaman and Pete share is that of obedience. (Oh man, I wish my editor hadn't had me add this chapter.) Although I have already opened my life up to some of my own serious character challenges, the character challenge of obedience steps on my toes regularly. (Oh, I hear you loud and clear on this one! "Ron, I could have done without this chapter as well." No, I'm not giving you the editor's name and address, that's all there is to it!)

Because both Naaman of old and Pete Rose of today were given much, much obedience was expected. This military great who expected obedience from his troops was now confronted as to whether or not he would obey God when it made no sense. However, after a little persuasion from the "hired help,"

Naaman chose to obey God's command that ran contrary to his military, logical mind and sure enough, after going under in a dirty river seven times as he was told to do, his leprous skin turned back to the texture of a "little child." Sadly the great Pete Rose's repentance came too late as far as allowing him to be inducted into the Hall of Fame.

I too was given much. So much that I have come to believe that if you are extremely talented and charismatic…it is almost a curse. Not really, but do you understand what I am trying to say? Having even just a fair amount of talent and ability makes it so easy to rely on yourself instead of God. Truth is, you can do it, at least most of the time. God will use the gifts He has given and receive glory even when we operate out of our own strength. One of the "quick sands of life" that is so easy to fall into when you are gifted and talented is that of "the rules are for everyone else but me." (Ouch!) Not to defend that attitude but you need to know that to a certain degree, if you fit into the category of which we are talking, much of it is thrust upon you. (You are still talking to me aren't you?) Without a doubt, if you are sharp, witty, funny, entertaining, and especially if you are great at sports, and possess even a little amount of smarts, doors will open that do not open for just everyone. Special perks will come your way without asking for them.

Somehow during an elongated season of unmet needs that produced great pain, I rationalized that it was okay to rewrite the rules. Having ceased trusting the Lord for those unmet needs, as well as not praising Him that He was Lord in the midst of the struggle, compromise was allowed into my life. The rules became skewed. As I have said earlier in the book, "I was wrong," under whatever the circumstance may have been. In case you do not realize it though, unmet needs and pain over an extended period of time will usually cause the best of us to have blurred vision to the rules, especially if you are outwardly successful.

The last church I pastored was exciting. For the first time in my pastoral ministry, we were actually "taking back some of the ground the devil had stolen." Our church was blessed with growth not because people were swapping churches but because people were genuinely coming to Christ. Within a short time, we had outgrown the church building and were meeting in the elementary school auditorium. We conducted the first evangelical crusade to take place outside a church building in that area. It was the first time an evangelist had ever spoken in the public schools. He was one of the few guys at the time who made me look "mainstream!" This guy wore a pair of pants made out of cowhide. On youth night, I felt like we needed to order enough pizza to feed 350 teenagers. Finding a pizza parlor that could handle that size order in that small town was tough. My secretary said, "Pastor, you need to realize this has never been done here before. If we have fifty kids show up it's going to be pretty serious." But I knew God had placed on my heart to order pizza for that number of kids. When we did a head count of those standing in line and counted just over 400, we quickly called in for more pizza.

With all of the hype of activity, the bottom line reason for the growth was because of a genuine move of the Spirit in which people not only were committing their lives to Christ, they were also growing in the knowledge of the Lord and marriages were strengthened. Well, a number of marriages were radically changed…but ours, it just did not happen. In fact, and this is a great example of spiritual warfare, after eighteen years of marriage, in the middle of preaching a series of messages on the home, I snapped. I just got tired of trying.

Let me pause for just a moment to speak to you whose marriage is not on solid ground. Note, I did not say to you who have a perfect or problem free marriage because that marriage does not exist. Nor am I talking to those of you who have suddenly found yourself in the weeds in your marriage and both of you are going to counseling, dealing with issues and crying out for God's help with an attitude of "whatever it takes to save our marriage, Lord we are willing," then you, my friend are on solid ground because all of heaven is lined up to help! God is on the side of marriage!

Here are a few ways to tell whether or not you are in the danger zone. Do you regularly battle thoughts of "If it wasn't that I'd lose everything I've worked for, I'd file for divorce in a heartbeat!" Or, is there someone of the opposite sex whom you really enjoy having one on one "planning sessions" with at work, church, the kids' school or little league? If this is you or anything close, please get help immediately! No matter what your status is or how much is resting on your ability to "keep things afloat," *nothing* is more important than your marriage and your children. I still believe most spouses when confronted in front of a third party, with a loving, humble spirit saying, "Honey, because I love you and our home, I fear that if *(fill in the blank)* continues, we may lose all that we hold near and dear and I do NOT want that to happen to us," then most spouses will respond positively even in the midst of hurt. Unfortunately I can tell you from experience that it would be much better for your spouse to hurt a little, comparatively, because you have spoken the truth in love about what is really going on within you, than to hurt them with an unbelievable amount of pain because you cannot take anymore and they discover after the fact the truth about you going off the deep end.

Back to the story! Life was good, outwardly. Feeling alone, isolated and still thinking, "I've got to keep this machine going," the rules became skewed and I bought the lie that it would be alright to live under one roof and have my emotional needs met under another. Was that the *spirit of stupid* or what?!? The enemy knew he could not get to me the way he did nine years prior so it was easy to rationalize, "but we're just talking," "we're just discussing situations that need attention at the church," (for you it may be the office), "our children are the same ages and we're just helping each other with child rearing issues." And here is the real *stinkin' thinkin'* : "this relationship is helping me survive!" For the record, I am not saying that we were so noble that had we been in a large metropolitan area it might not have turned into a physical relationship, but due to living in a smaller area where I was high profile, there was no way that was going to happen. Another satanic rationalization was that it was not that bad because we were not at all thinking of doing something really stupid like running off or divorcing our spouses to do so. However it was just as wrong, ugly, and sinful as if it had been a physical affair.

Because our Heavenly Daddy loves us so much, he will only allow us to go so far until He says, "that's enough!" And just like the writer of Hebrews talks about how none of us like to be spanked…ah but are we not glad that He loves us so much that He will not allow us to remain as we are? The day came when my beloved youth pastor, of whom I am so proud, confronted both of us separately. Although I was truthful and honest and admitted the wrong, it had to be dealt with. To whom much is given, much is expected. In less than forty-five days from that confrontation, I had resigned from the church, we left our beloved Colorado, we returned to our home town, and my marriage of twenty years was in ruins. After spending two weeks at the *Retreat for Pastors in Crisis* counseling center, we were determined to keep our marriage together. I had immediately entered the initial stages of repentance begging for forgiveness, yet upon our return home my wife obviously had her reasons for leaving. I was benched and broken!

Looking through the "help wanted" ads, I could not find one single ad that read, "Wanted, washed up preacher, $75,000 per year." I was so depressed. It was after a couple of months that Bob Duane, to whom this book is dedicated, called and asked if I wanted to come to Dallas and square away his customer service department at US Foodservice. What began as a two week stint of staying with his precious family turned into six months at his house and just over a year in Dallas. Someone had to keep the financial boat afloat and with three teenagers, it took both of us to do that. Although the offer was made for all of us to move to Dallas, it was rejected. The Duane family lived in Grapevine and the warehouse was in Mesquite. Many a morning during what I now affectionately refer to as my "Dark Days of Dallas," I was crying the entire fifty minute drive to work. Listening to *Jon Rivers and the Morning Gang* on KLTY became part of my sustenance. Each day I *had* to hear Phillips, Craig, and Dean singing *Mercy Came Running* because I felt like the scumbag of the universe. I *had* to hear

Greg Long sing *These Are the Days of Grace* because I needed to be reminded that God's grace and forgiveness were all over me. And Geoff and Aaron Benward's song, *After the Rain*, reassured me that the sun would shine again in my life. For nearly that entire year, I stayed parked in Psalms and Proverbs reading of how "His love endures forever." The weekend after Thanksgiving I was all alone in the Duane's house when God did a "hat dance" on my heart. He showed me in no uncertain terms that while I had been fiercely honest while preaching the Word, I had been dishonest when dealing with people close to me. While I did not lie, I did not speak the truth that they needed to hear because I did not want to offend them. Plus, and here is the real "gut wrencher," He spoke to me as to how having your "loins covered in truth" was more than just not telling lies, it was living a lifestyle of truth. Our loins are right at the center of our bodies. In other words, at the very center of our very being should be truth.

Although I was benched and broken, a great amount of joy came over me when I got to the point of saying, "Lord, even if I never preach again, I can still be a witness!" The times I met with my nephew David at a Waffle House to share the Word and find out what God was doing in his life brought me to a point of understanding that big crowds and lots of noise are not "where it's at." Joni and Rolando Pupo modeled this for me. Not only did I experience their love for me, but I observed it during their Sunday morning Bible study class in which they are not afraid to veer off course of the lesson in order to minister to someone who is hurting. This petite blond and her husband from Cuba have touched literally hundreds of lives as they continue to teach the Word and love on and pray for hurting people.

After nearly a year, I could no longer be away from my children. Trying so hard not to miss any paychecks, I thought I had found something solid when I returned to Oklahoma City. Wrong! Finally, I accepted a sales job from a small company who had just acquired the distributorship for an interactive television video game. Now the game in and of itself is legal, moral, and ethical. However, the fact of the matter is that only the bars could afford them. Suddenly I found myself in places that I had never been in before. Plus, as I was trying to sell these fun little gizmos, I was thinking, "You know Buddy, I hope you go out of business," and that just does not make for good "sales energy."

As I began to come out of my season of being disciplined, I once again began to realize that although God had benched me from public ministry, He had not benched public ministry from me. If it were not for Romans 11:29, that specifically says "the gifts and callings of God are irrevocable," I am certain I would have thrown in the towel. Knowing precisely what your gifts are and that God has not changed His mind about giving them to you is hugely important.

In college I wrote and produced radio commercials for a home center that I built a carpet business for. One of the many successes that I had while pastoring was writing and voicing creative radio spots. One day the thought hit me, "I can do that! I believe I could do that for television as well as the on camera talent." After finding an agent, I began making television commercials. During this early stage of being restored, I even walked into an independent television station and asked to talk with the General Manager. After sitting down in his office, I proceeded to tell him that I wrote and produced television commercials and could even be the talent if he needed me to be. Surprise, surprise, he looked across his desk and asked, "You could do that?" My response was of course, "Yes sir!" He went on to tell me that they actually needed a couple made and asked how much would I charge him to write, produce, and appear in them. Mercy, I was not ready for him to ask *that!* I had never made a dime off of any of the radio spots I had ever done. The Lord gave me the right words when I said, "Well, I like to find out what each client's needs are and customize a price according to the project."

One thing led to another. I was even the star of a late night Home Shopping Network Wannabe show. Plus, there was a season of promoting and bringing Christian concerts to town even though at the time we did not have an Adult Contemporary Christian music station in town. Few people knew the difference between Crystal Lewis and Crystal Gayle and did I ever loose my shirt. One fall, I was just about to pack up and move to either Nashville or Colorado Springs. With so many evangelical publications coming from these two cities, I felt as though I could get on with some organization and become a staff writer. It was at that time that K-LOVE Radio of Sacramento, California, purchased the radio station owned by Oklahoma Christian University. My thought was that I could use a few more coins before heading out and with my public relation skills combined with my knowledge of Contemporary Christian music, *maybe* they could use someone as a point person at least temporarily to get their name out. But God had other plans! Mr. Lloyd Parker, the General

Manager at that time, was and still is a genuine "God-send" in my life. He wanted to talk to me about coming on full time. At the time I had two and a half kids in college and thought, "a steady income rather than the feast or famine might be nice," and thus began a seven year ride in which I had NO idea as to how God was going to use it to put me back out in front of people, sharing His love. Lloyd and I were about as evenly matched as Simon the Zealot who lived, ate, breathed, and slept the overthrow of the Roman Empire and Matthew the Tax Collector who worked for the Roman Government. Lloyd is a bona fide Yankee who lived most of his life on Long Island. As a boy from the Bible Belt, I was not sure if the Gospel had even reached Long Island yet! Whereas I still have a "hundred years of down home running through my blood." Can I say that there is at least still some residue of "red" on my neck? But for some reason, Lloyd believed in me and stood by me, and after the first couple of years of learning how to work together, to this day I count him a close friend and a fellow comrade for the cause of Christ. Without a doubt, God blessed my ministry with K-LOVE beyond my wildest dreams. Not long after we went on the air, I needed a local television show to promote a Kathy Troccoli concert. Steve Easom, who had hired me the year before to write, produce, and appear in my first television commercial, pointed me towards the *Higher Life with Sammi* show. During that appearance, Sammi and I hit it off so well on camera that she and her husband Charles, who produced and directed the show, asked me to come back as a regular co-host. When God brought me back this time, instead of being in front of a few hundred, He put me in front of thousands.

If you are currently going through a season or if you find

yourself someday going through a time of being benched and broken…accept it! The scripture in Proverbs 3:11 talks about not rejecting the discipline of the Lord. During a season of brokenness it is alright for business not to be "as usual." You will need extra time to heal and just sit and listen to what God has to say to you through His Word. It has been accurately said that God cannot fix what is not broken and will not use the vessel that has not been broken.

God did not call you to sit on the bench the rest of your life. Nail down his calling and gifts that He has placed within you. Seek His vision for your life and join Him. Be cautious not to return to the game too soon but when the great Coach of the Universe tells you to get ready to bat, do not hesitate to step up to the plate. Whether it is a business venture, a romantic relationship, or mending a relational fence, if God says it is time to get back in the game, it is a *certainty* that you will not be happy sitting on the bench.

BENCHED does not = BANNED from the game for LIFE
BROKEN means NOW God can FIX what needs FIXING

CHAPTER 9

WHEN YOU'VE STRUCK OUT FOR WHAT FEELS LIKE THE LAST TIME

Principle Number 9: TENACIOUSLY hold on 2 Your Faith

Pastoring small churches when the children were small meant that we learned to enjoy the small but special events in life. Sometimes we could afford them. Sometimes we could not. Sometimes we shared two soft drinks between all five of us. On occasion, however, we each got an ice cream cone of our own. But again, there were times when we could not afford to stop. Even as the "wee-three" would passionately say, "Daddy, Daddy, can we stop and get an ice cream cone," although it was hard to say, "no," there were those times that it had to be said. As small children there was no way they could understand the reality of not being able to afford a frozen delight. They "thought as a child." Their thoughts were not my thoughts.

It was just another hot summer Sunday morning in 2000 on my way to the Singles Bible Study Class after the second service. Being the *rather strange* person that I am and feeling more comfortable on stage in front of 12,000 people at an arena than a Sunday School class of twenty, I got fidgety

HOW TO KEEP SWINGING...

when the class did not get started as quickly as I thought it should have. And with the knowledge that flavored coffee was to be found out the door and across the main foyer of the church auditorium, how could I sit still? Although I did not *need* the coffee, mind you, I just wanted to enjoy the *taste* of another cup during class. And since people were still making small talk, I decided to go for it. How could I have known how this trip to get a cup of coffee would be the beginning of an unforgettable ride?

As I came upon the crowded foyer with people filing into the worship center, my eyes caught a vision. Praise the Lord, where had this woman been all my life? Who was this woman in line to enter the third service? Why had I never seen her before? I am just telling you now, I was "all shook up!" I had to find out if anyone knew who she was. I even went out to what I thought was going to be a singles luncheon which turned out to be three married couples and the girl who had invited me. But I thought surely, since these folks had been in the church longer than I, with an accurate description of this heavenly creature, surely they could tell me who she was.

Nope, she did not "ring a bell" in the minds of any of them. However, approximately three Sundays later as I was exiting the second service, she appeared again, already in her seat about three quarters of the way back in the center section that I just *happened* to be walking by. Being the "Southern Gentleman" that I am, along with the good church member that I try to be, I had a deep concern that just in case she was just visiting the church, I did not want to neglect my duty in welcoming her to the service. With great confidence, I introduced myself and asked her if she was a guest.

Approximately seven months from our meeting, I dropped to my knees, on stage, in front of 2500 people at a concert with a engagement ring in hand and asked this "princess" from Afghanistan for her hand in marriage. It was a total of only fourteen months from our first official meeting on my way out of church that, after an on again/off again courtship and engagement period, we publicly said our commitment to marriage in front of friends and family. Due to my friends in the media and the September 11th attacks on our nation, we were interviewed on two local news stations and written up in the newspaper.

We danced in step with each other. I was so proud to be seen with this beautiful lady. Although there were challenges, well into the third year my heart still melted when I looked at her. She possessed an inward beauty and intellect that transcended her outward appearance. We lived in a new house in a gated community with great neighbors. I was happier and more fulfilled than ever before in my life.

On the day after Christmas in 2003, the state of Oklahoma was shaken by the murder of one of its finest Highway Patrol Officers. This sharp young husband and father of three precious little girls was also the Youth Pastor at a small, rural church not far from the southwestern Oklahoma K-LOVE Radio city of license. Feeling certain that they would be K-LOVE listeners, my wife and I went to this church only two days after his murder to love on them and assure them of our support as well as the prayers of the K-LOVE listening audience. When we met the Officer's widow and three small daughters whom he left behind, our hearts broke. As friendship was established, I took this church, and its pastor, that was absolutely rocked by this happening under my wing. Three days after this senseless murder, I was on the K-LOVE Radio Network asking nearly three million people to pray for this family and church.

Less than ninety days after this life altering event occurred, we returned to this small community for a special service in which I was scheduled to speak. This turned out to be a big deal due to my affiliation with the radio station. The church was packed with kids sitting of the floor, people standing around the walls, and people standing outside, looking in the front door. The presence of God was so real during that special service. People were touched and born again before the service was over.

At this point I must pause and do a "set up" for what was about to become the most bizarre period of my life, thus far. If you think of satanic attacks as being primarily on the drug pusher, prostitute, or pornography peddler, think again! I am convinced that the enemy does not waste too much of his time on people whom he has wrapped around his finger. It is the folks who are moving in God's direction for their lives whom he makes an all out effort to trip up.

In the midst of this Holy Spirit anointed service, the enemy absolutely attacked my wife. As we walked out from that special night in which people were standing around fellowshipping in the afterglow, she was livid! This precious woman whom I had committed my heart to thought that there was something going on between the recently bereaved widow and me. No amount of reasoning as to how I was committed to our marriage, reassuring her of my love, or asking why would I want mess my life up *again*, made any headway in calming her down. When we returned home after a two-and-a-half hour drive, this precious woman, whom I thought to be my soul mate, threw her wedding ring down and said, "It's *over!*"

Sleeping in separate rooms, the rage continued for several days. On the third day, I called the couple whom I mentioned in Chapter 5, who conduct the marriage workshops and counseling ministry. Wouldn't you know it? They were on their East Coast tour! But he put us on speaker phone and infused what turned out to be only a temporary calm to the storm, but a "calm" nevertheless. This "calm" lasted for only about twenty-nine hours. It was after a two hour Sunday afternoon nap in which she awakened in a rage, CONVINCED that this recently bereaved widow who lived two-and-a-half hours away, mother of three young girls who was trying to keep a youth group going, was driving to our house, four days a week, so that she and I could commit adultery in our marriage bed.

Hold on to your seats, this story is going downhill from here! Not only was I accused of infidelity, she up and filed for divorce only seven days after I preached the great service of which I wrote. Yes, the enemy attacked even further. On the eighth day after the special night at the church, I received a phone call. Her voice was frantic as she informed me of how she had figured out that I had a plan to murder her and marry the widow in question and that she was going to be the "pastor's wife" that I had always wanted! Although, as you have read, I have done a lot of wrong and have been accused of a lot of wrongdoing, I had never been accused of that! I will never forget being in my car and barely able to breathe after hearing

HOW TO KEEP SWINGING...

this accusation. The only response I could muster was, "Oh, honey, that is so bizarre."

Calling on my close prayer warrior friends, I was *not* going to let the devil destroy this marriage. Much warfare in the spirit realm was done. When she came one Sunday afternoon to get her belongings from the house, she found ninety different, handwritten "I love you" signs with scriptures written at the bottom plastered all around the house that love had built. During this separation period, to my dismay, there were only four or five phone conversations and a consistent refusal to come together for counseling sessions. For eight months, I stood fast knowing that a miracle was on the way. During this bizarre time in which no amount of reasoning by myself or friends could change her heart in the least, yet God worked big time in my life. He revealed numerous areas in which His "heavenly sandpaper" was needed. He taught me to abstain from *any* appearance of impropriety, as I kept my wedding ring on my left hand during this entire time. I praised, prayed, wept, and sat alone many nights in our beautiful house. It was also a definite blessing to have four Godly men who encouraged me and kept me accountable. Gerald Deaton, a dear brother from San Diego would call morning and night to pray with me and see how I was doing. Let me also say that it was such a good feeling this time to be able to say to the Senior Pastor of the K-LOVE Radio ministry that I was a part of, "I have nothing to hide, I am fully accountable, feel free to ask me any cold hard question you want!"

During this season, there were some unique challenges that accompanied being high profile and in the spotlight when one of life's storms hits. Appearances at concerts, bookstores, and churches were already scheduled. The ball was in motion and whether I felt like it or not, I had to go out with a smile and focus on the job at hand. God was so good during this time (as He always is) to not only surround me with His presence, but to cause me to realize that the greatest way to "get back at" the devil was to lift up the name of Jesus! The Sundays that I was not speaking or doing something for the radio ministry were especially tough, due to being in between churches as far as membership goes. After having worked with so many of our churches here in the Oklahoma City area and being known as married, it was quite difficult to find a church where I was not either asked, "where is your wife," being recognized as the "K-LOVE Guy," or being asked for an autograph.

After my initial appearances were completed, however, I was able to take some time off from the spotlight. For ninety days, I was not heard from in person or on the air. During this time, I was able to go to a precious pastor and explain what I was going through. I told him, "Look, I need a church that I can attend without being the 'K-LOVE Guy,' where I can just sit and be ministered to." It was shortly after this brief period I that believe the Lord told me, "Okay, it's time to pick yourself up and go out and do what you do best, which is to love on this city. Go and reinvent yourself." As a result, we began touring central Oklahoma, having special "K-LOVE Days" at local churches. We promoted that day on the airwaves, I delivered the message, and brought a local artist along with a praise band that would lead the praise and worship time. Those days turned out to be one day revivals in those churches.

After eight months, the miracle that I believed for did not happen. Our "legal" divorce became final. Yes, I most definitely felt as though I had "struck out" for the last time! Did God fail? Absolutely not! He knew what He was doing! His thoughts were not my thoughts. Was it his will that this precious woman allowed this deception to destroy our marriage? Absolutely not! Does He allow events and circumstances that are not His will to happen in order to accomplish His will? Absolutely![66]

Right about now, I am hearing you again! You are asking, "How do you *Keep Swinging When You've Struck Out for What Feels Like The Last Time?*" First of all, you cry out in honesty to Jesus. If you are feeling pain, despair, or anger. If you just want to scream, "Lord I *hate* this time," be honest with your Heavenly Daddy.[67] Then in the very next breath, with all of the Holy Spirit strength that He will give you, pick up the baseball bat of praise and begin giving Him thanks and praise. Whether you feel like it or not! In fact, you very well may not feel like praising Him. There is nowhere in scripture in which we are commanded to trust, praise, and worship our mighty God when we feel like it. As a matter of fact, we are commanded in 1 Thessalonians 5:18, "in everything give thanks; for this is God's will for you in Christ Jesus."

Okay, hit me with your best shot! Some of you are saying, "Now wait just a cotton pickin' minute!" (Cotton pickin' is of course a good Baptist cuss phrase). "Ron, I thought you said that there are events and circumstances that are absolutely not His will?!?" *Oh dear enquiring mind*, let us look at the punctuation in this verse. Do you see the semi-colon there? This verse is not saying that everything is God's will for us. Rather, this verse is saying it is His will that we give thanks in everything.

With each phrase of praise that you can lift up, especially

after striking out in a marriage, a business deal, with your children, or finances, God will begin giving you the gumption to step up to the plate of life with a fresh grip and swing the bat once again! Even if you just begin by giving thanks that you "woke up on this side of the dirt" this morning, begin now to praise Him. Like my sweet momma who was called home last year always said, "We've got so much to be thankful for!"

I can honestly say to you as I write this book that I know what it is to get happy and rejoice in the Lord when experiencing a "medium-well done New York cut steak" of life. At the same time, if I could look you in the eyes (I'm certain someone, somewhere is working on a high tech gadget to insert in books where the author can look at who is reading the book), I would tell you that I also know what it is to get happy and rejoice in the Lord while experiencing one of life's "peanut butter sandwich"[68] times thinking, "This is it! I'll never be allowed to step up to the plate again!"

The fact that you are reading this book is something to be thankful for. Did you wake up this morning, having slept in a bed last night? If not, did you sleep on the floor with a roof over your head? Have you had the opportunity to eat at least one meal in the last twenty-four hours? Even if you are saying, "The pitch that I swung at was so stupid that my friends and family have all walked away," I want you to know Jesus has not walked away, NOR has He given up on you.[70]

Jeremiah 29:11, "For I know the plans that I have for you, declares the Lord, plans for welfare and not for calamity to give you a future and a hope," was written to those *Crazy Kids of Israel*, during one of their darkest times. In fact, this was spoken to them as many of them were being led off into captivity with grappling hooks in their lips. Even if you are being sent to the dugout, the locker room, or thrown out of the game, it is only temporary. God has used those times in my life to sharpen me and for me to plug into what He is doing, along with getting His fresh vision for my welfare and future.

Okay, maybe I have been a little wordy so far as to what to do when you *really think* it is all over. SO I will attempt to write faster. Shortly after you have struck out and have sat down in the dugout, remember to be honest with God about your feelings then take a moment to regroup and begin to enter into His presence with praise and thanksgiving.

Thirdly, trust. Your Heavenly Daddy knows what He is doing, you probably do not. One time in the late '80's, I thought that we needed to move to the Dallas/Ft. Worth area so that I could finish seminary. Plus I was of the mindset that if I was going to re-enter full time evangelism, I needed to live in that particular Metro-plex. The house we rented had a neat little covered back porch, just the right height in which to conduct my "School of Trust," for the "wee-three." I knew this would help them conquer fear as they learned to trust their earthly daddy and someday this would transcend into helping them trust their Heavenly Daddy.

This "high tech" school consisted of setting each one of them on top of the over hang of this porch and having them jump to me. Children are a hoot! Are they not? Jessica, our youngest and most tender (to this day still) was the "dare-devil" out of the three. She jumped into my arms the first time. Although I cannot remember exactly, I believe that it took David a couple of tries to muster up the courage. Jennifer, however, took several weekends, but it was so cool when

I walked through the door one Friday evening and she proclaimed, "Daddy, I'm ready to jump!" Mentally, she had already conquered the fear and trusted that her daddy would in fact catch her when she took that "leap of faith."

Just as our precious babies learned to trust that their daddy would catch them and not allow them to damage themselves, please know that you can absolutely trust that your Heavenly Daddy will not allow you to fall so hard that you become "damaged goods." Note, I am in no way saying that you may not *feel* like damaged goods. We can, however, without a doubt trust that when the Father allows tragedy, enacts discipline, or lets you experience rejection it is not to damage you. As much as it hurt, I *knew* that I knew that I could "trust His heart" even in this situation of being falsely accused. One of my four close friends and accountability partners told me of how her rejection just very well may have been God's protection.

After eight long months of "faithing it out" for a miracle, it did not happen. Although I wrestled for months afterwards as to "why" and "what all of the faith was about," I came to this conclusion:

"Faith makes sense, even when life does not,
Faith makes sense, when Jesus is all you've got,
To believe in what you cannot see,
To become all you were made to be,
Faith makes sense, faith makes sense,
Faith in Him, makes sense!"

My faith did not change the circumstances, but it did change me. As stated, there were those down days, but overall I had a higher walk due to having a focus on the presence and purpose of God in my life.

In fact, this instance reminded me of the summer that I turned fourteen. We were moving from our nice new, four bedroom house in the neighborhood where the "cool kids" lived into one of my parents' remodeled but enlarged rent houses in a not so "cool kids" neighborhood. Even with all of my whining, asking, "Why do we have to move over there when all of the cool kids live here," my daddy was resolute in his purpose for the move. "Ronnie, I want to get out of debt." He knew what he was doing. I did not. I could not! I was after all, only fourteen. Nowadays, after all of these years, I can certainly appreciate the concept of being out of debt. Through the years, as this house has been a refuge when my life has gotten out of whack, I have been able to see that my daddy did in fact know what he was doing.

Psalm 46:10 says, "Be still and know that I am God…" The Hebrew states, "Let go, relax and know that I am God."… and you're not!" (Obviously the "and you're not" is the RMRV addition.) After all of the kicking, screaming, and pitching a fit in general that we may do, the Father is resolute in His purpose of making us holy. When we come to the point of "just chillin," letting go of our expectations, and knowing that He is God, (i.e. a force much more powerful that is able to break our own will who is much more committed to our good than are we) and that we are not (cause if we were we would make a mess at being God, remember what happened in the movie "Bruce Almighty?), we will then and only then experience the "peace that (totally) passes (all) understanding."

After you have cried out to Jesus, continually offered up the "sacrifice of praise,"[71] and made the choice to trust Him, just know that He has not called an emergency session of the

Trinity concerning what may feel like is your very last "chance at bat." Knowing that there has never been a conversation in the heavenly realm with a dialogue of "Oh my gosh, did you see what Ron Moore has done now?! What are we going to do with the boy now?!? You got any ideas Son? How about You, Holy Spirit? How in the world are we going to pull off the plan we've had for him now?!?"

Never has this type of conversation taken place concerning your life either. Knowing that your Heavenly Daddy has the situation of our lives under control means that I can and you can stay in the game, believing that God still has great days ahead for our lives.

> When U R Sitting On the Bench REALIZE That As Long As U Have Breath Almighty God Will Give U Strength If You Will Let Him to Step Up to Whatever Plate U Need To For Each New Day

CHAPTER 10

Beware of the Teammates You Choose

Principle Number 10: The teammates U choose 2-Day R the 1's U will PROBABLY have 2 live with 2-morrow

Shortly after Election Day in November of 1988, we somewhat slithered back to our beloved Denver, Colorado. After yet another bad experience with church people who had promised us the moon in a particularly small town pastorate in Nebraska and physically did not deliver dirt, my attitude was not the greatest to say the least. (Ahh, the wisdom of Jennifer who was only eleven when she made the profound statement, "Daddy, people don't move to towns like this, they move out of towns like this.") My thoughts were, *my finances and the welfare of my family will never be left in the hands of church people again!* Therefore bells rang and lights flashed when "Doug Cheatem" offered me a way to go into the printing business for myself. When I said that I did not know anything about printing, his response was that the "Flash Copy" philosophy was that you could always hire a press operator, they wanted a promoter at the helm. Music to my ears! "Promotions-R-Me" has been one of my "life themes" for a *long* time! The deal was to build one of his "Flash Copy" locations and "by golly," he would work out a deal for me to buy the business.

Now please understand Doug and Shelia Cheatem were good Baptist folks from Texas. Why would I have needed to get anything in writing? Doug's brother was even a pastor "for Pete's sake!" (Please contact me immediately if you know which "Pete" it is who has so much done for his sake.)

Shortly after we had shaken hands on this deal, I was sent to the "Flash Copy" franchise headquarters for training. Over the next year and a half, I poured myself into learning the printing business and building what I thought would become our "family business." Opportunities to preach on Sundays and Wednesdays opened and life was generally good. One night after about eighteen months, the Cheatems even took us out to dinner to ask us if we were committed over the long haul to continue to build the business. Our answer without hesitation was, "Yes, of course!" Unfortunately, I never thought to ask them if they were still committed to our agreement!

In less than two weeks after that dinner, one Monday morning, Doug walked into the "Flash Copy" print shop and caught me by total surprise when he announced that I needed to clean out my desk because I was no longer needed. And, of course, he wanted the keys to the company car returned as well. "But, but, I built the business!" Didn't matter, he was still legally the sole proprietor and could do as he wished with his business.

Once again we were plunged into financial and emotional hardship in which the Cheatems refused to even allow me to draw unemployment. The year of 1990 will live in infamy in the history of our family. By the end of that year, we had not only lost the business that our hopes and dreams were set on as becoming ours, but because of financial hardship, we also lost the house we loved. Not to mention the church we were a part of had a major split and ran off our beloved pastor, and by years end we did not even have a car to drive!

Although I never want to stop believing in people, I am certain there is wisdom in choosing those whom you play this game of life with. Whether it is a serious position such as marriage or business partner, the friends that you hang with, or the church you attend, all of these and other key positions in the game will have a tremendous effect as to how soon or whether or not you accomplish all that your Heavenly Daddy has set forth for you to accomplish. Now, now, I am hearing the mutterings under your breath! "Well what's meant to be will be, will it not?!?"

Romans 8:28, which has been mentioned numerous times throughout this book talking about how "all things" are working together for our good, is not the catalyst scripture for what I call "Doris Day Theology." You know the song that she made famous (or well…if you are under forty, on second thought, you probably will not, but humor me, will you?), "Que Sera, Sera, whatever will be, will be. The future's (come on sing along) not ours to see. Que Sera, Sera…" While this makes for a good song, it is bad theology! In fact, in philosophical circles it is known as "fatalism." Untold millions of events happen every day, all around the globe that are not the will of God. All the way from aborted babies, hungry children, broken marriages, children who are molested, adultery, to murder, and absolutely none of these are the will of our Heavenly

Daddy. The fact that God allows these tragedies to happen does in no way mean that they are His will![72]

For too long, in many Christian circles, we have elevated stupidity! As I was leading in a verse by verse study through the book of Proverbs a few years ago, I became absolutely convinced that God's will is for His children to walk in wisdom! How many times have I heard brothers or sisters stand and testify (in a Roy D. Mercer style voice) something similar to, "Glory to God, I was driving my car when all of the sudden Praise the Lord, the engine went out! Smoke was coming out everywhere, hallelujah, when I realized that I hadn't checked the oil in 35,000 miles amen! And after I told the tow truck driver that 'Jesus paid it all' and that he could keep the car, glory to God, the Lord laid it on the heart of the person who I asked if they wouldn't mind givin' me a ride twenty miles, out of their way, one way to work each day to donate a $500.00 Lincoln Continental, praise the Lord, He knows how to provide!"

God's will is for us check the oil before our engine burns up. Almighty God who founded the earth, "by wisdom,"[73] is not into the "spirit of stupid!" And please allow me to espouse yet another deep spiritual truth, "stupid begets stupid!" However, "he who walks with the wise will himself be wise."[74] This is why it is so key for us to choose teammates who are wise. Wisdom begets wisdom. Smart decisions usually beget smart decisions. Although we are not total products of our environment, i.e. if allowed, God will give us the ability to break away from teams who are negative and self destructive, as long as we continue to play on their teams they will have a tremendous influence on us.

"Why is this," you ask? Simply put, (get ready, here comes a Bible principle) because the voice and/or voices that we listen to are going to win whatever battle we face. They will influence whatever decision there is to make. "Wisdom" dictated that I should have said something to the effect of, "Doug Cheatem, I appreciate so much your belief in me and our friendship. But so as to avoid any misunderstandings, why don't you draw something up in writing as to what is actually expected of me and where the print shop needs to be in monthly sales in order for us to make this transaction." (Yes, I realize we cannot live our lives in the "should-a, would-a, could-a realm, I use this for illustrative purposes only.)

Please know that I am not trying to be cruel when I use the following illustrations. If you surround yourself with men who look at pornography and are constantly undressing women in their mind, cheating on your wife will not be that difficult of a decision to make. Nor will it be offensive to the guys you run with. If you are obese and have teammates who consistently overeat and do not exercise, overeating and being slovenly will be an easy choice. If you are still in the process of completing your formal education and are a part of study groups who accept cheating as a way of life, there will come a time in which you will not give cheating on your taxes a second thought. If you are a female surrounded by women who accept gossip, are rebellious towards their husbands, demanding, and in general are hard to get along with, then choosing to have that type of marriage relationship will not be hard to do. If you constantly hang with people who ignite the fires of complaining about your spouse and easily spout off with a "well you ought to leave him/her," get ready to take a major hit!

We all need those two or three close friends who say to us as my close friend Jon Cook said to me one time, "Are you *crazy?!?*"

The habits and actions that are tolerated by our friends and family will most often become the accepted norm for our lives. This is why I tell singles, "Check out your potential spouse's teammates. Who are the friends they run with? What do they do for fun?" If your significant other's close inner circle of friends are into forms of recreation that are obviously immoral and in direct opposition to either a Bible specific or a Bible principle, the wedding event will not suddenly change them!

Although scripture does have many "black and whites," there are those areas that scripture is not specific on, and one of the greatest nuggets of wisdom that has stayed with me is from Dr. Ralph Wilkerson when he said, "We can only be dogmatic on what the scripture is dogmatic on." However, there are so many choices and decisions that fall under the category of wisdom. "Frinstance," (as my high school English teacher Mrs. Anderson used to say) the Bible does not specifically say, "Thou shall not smoke." However, it does not take "a spiritual batting average of a 1000" to figure out that the body was not designed to operate efficiently with smoke being sucked into it over a period of years. The Bible does not mention a thing about watching hours of mindless television. Wisdom dictates that if you spend your evenings in front of the "boob tube," you probably will not be focusing your mind on "things that are above and not of this world."[75] Are you getting the picture?

The book of Proverbs speaks over and over about seeking wisdom. "Seeking!" Not waiting for it to come and hit us upside the head. One time I heard my fellow Marine Dr. Chuck Swindoll say, "I've never seen a wise young person. I've seen a number of smart young people. A number of sharp young people, but wisdom comes with years." The ability to make wise decisions, however, does not depend on our age only. Here again, the will of God is not that we continue to strike out, get benched, and thrown out of the game until we are old and have mental arthritis before we have wisdom. Unfortunately that happens far too often. One example out of Proverbs is seeking wisdom as if it is a prized treasure.[76] How much time do most of us spend seeking just enough treasure to pay our bills? The scripture goes on to say that having wisdom is better than having a lot of money, yet how much time do we spend genuinely seeking wisdom versus money?

I have been so blessed in my life to know two men who sought wisdom as young men, Dr. Ronnie Floyd, Senior Pastor of the great First Baptist Church of Springdale, Arkansas and Bobby Duane, a hugely successful business man in the Dallas/Ft.Worth Metro-plex. I had the privilege of getting to know both of these men in their early twenties and observed how they were teachable. They did not "know it all" like so many of us. They both sought counsel in making wise decisions, in choosing teammates, and before stepping up to the plate and swinging at the first ball that came along. They listened to some men who had already hit a homerun or two, or three, or four.

If you are feeling like the "village idiot in the body of Christ" because you have made so many stupid decisions and are surrounded by teammates who accept the status quo with a negative defeatist attitude, as soon as possible, seek wisdom! The letter that James, the half brother of Jesus, wrote tells us that God will give us wisdom if we will ask for it.[77] And when we do finally ask, he describes how the Lord will not say, "Wait a minute, that twerp's not done what I asked in the past, I think I'll just let him go about his stupid ways!" No, that is not the way our Heavenly Daddy operates. In fact, this is an example where Almighty God can be described as a liberal, because this passage goes on to say that He will give us wisdom, "liberally!"

"Ask" and "seek," both of these are keys to attaining wisdom. Many of us want God to just "zap" us so that we will never be bothered by "stupid" of any kind ever again. This mindset is not uncommon in the quick and easy society in which we live. The ninety seconds it takes to "Dial-Up" our connection to the internet in order to be connected to people, businesses, and information all around the globe is just too slow, we have to have high-speed! We get beside ourselves if our phone call fifteen hundred miles across country takes longer than five seconds to ring! If one fast food line is too long, we will go across the street to the next one because *we want what we want and we want it now*!

Although there are times in which God may give us a "word of wisdom"[78] about a particular situation or person, wisdom in general, being wise (not to be confused with a "wise-guy"), is a result of a lifestyle of asking as well as seeking. "No, Virginia," there is no such person who has been, nor is there any Bible promise of being zapped with wisdom. Neither does our age guarantee wisdom. You have probably heard the old saying, "there's no fool like an old fool!" Unfortunately the gray of our hair that so many of we "baby-boomers" try to cover does not automatically mean that we have wisdom.

If you have even the least desire in continuing to step up to the game of life and make some "hits" rather than take some "hits," the time to begin asking and seeking wisdom is now! Are you spending at least fifteen to thirty minutes alone in God's Word five or six days a week? If not, begin there with reading and meditating on the ultimate "book of wisdom." If your inner-circle of friends are not people who are moving in the direction of wisdom, re-evaluate those relationships. You will most likely need to find new friends who are moving in wisdom's direction along with those who possess an insatiable desire to step up to the "plate of life," as long as they have breath to breathe.

Reassess who and what you listen to. Remember, "garbage in, garbage out!" Although there are times for relaxing, reading, and watching mindless television to unwind, make certain that the majority of what goes in to the great recorder of your mind not only challenges you to be all God has called you to be, but increases your knowledge in many different areas. The books we read need to call us to wisdom.

Even if you are fifty years of age or over, it is not too late to begin operating with wisdom in your personal relationships, business dealings, or with your family. If you are currently on the bench in the dugout, it is not the will of your Heavenly Daddy for you to stay there the remainder of your days.

In 1981, I was fired from a church staff by one of the "BTE's" for not making the quota of families joining the church that he felt should be joining. Our baby girl Jessica had recently arrived, so the need for a paying job was paramount. Upon the recommendation of a friend, I went to some members of our church who were the "and Sons" of the William E. Davis and Sons Institutional Food Distribution Company. What is now known as the "blue van days" turned out to be a memorable time in our young family. I would usually take one of the two older kids with me on long hauls as I made special "hot-shot" deliveries. One afternoon as I was talking to Charles Davis, the youngest of the "and Sons," his dad, William E., called his office. He quickly got off the call, arose from his desk and said, "I've got to go see my dad, he probably wants to chew me out!" In another one of those rare moments that I was listening, God spoke! Clear as a bell, He said, "That's your position!" With great profundity, I responded with a, "Huh?" In another one of those rare times in which I can say, "I know that I know" God spoke to me, He told me that afternoon, "That is your position. When Charles Davis goes in to be chewed out by his dad, he's not afraid for one second that his father who has groomed him, educated him and personally trained him, would fire him or banish him to the deep freezer (a huge section of a food warehouse) to work on the fork lift for the rest of his life! Charles Davis is one of the "and sons." His name is on the sign! Yes, that is your position!"[79]

What he spoke to me during that brief moment caused me to see more clearly of our position *if* we are truly a "son" or "daughter" of the Lord Jesus. We may have swung at a ball that is high and outside time and time again and have had to be on the bench so often that the bench has an indentation of our rear end. The bench, however, is *not* where our Heavenly Daddy intends for us to spend the rest of our lives between now and the time He calls us home to Heaven. After all, He sent His only begotten Son to die on the cross and gave us the pledge of His Holy Spirit to indwell us so that we could ultimately win over every situation in this life. Remember, your contract was purchased with a high price and He did not choose you to be on His team so that you could warm a bench.

Right now, if you need to confess "stupid" to God, family or friends, do it immediately and begin asking the Head Coach, your Heavenly Daddy, for wisdom. Learn to make seeking wisdom a lifestyle. There is no doubt, if you have been born again by the Spirit of God, you have the power to begin a walk of wisdom![80]

Do U need to make changes in the roster of your life? If so, do it quickly!

CHAPTER 11

PRAYER–THE LOADED BAT OF THIS LIFE

Principle Number 11: U CAN X-perience SUPERNATURAL Power

Shortly after high school, I was speaking at a "revival meeting" in a church just east of Oklahoma City. As a flaming teenage evangelist, I was tremendously concerned about knocking on doors and visiting in homes, at swimming pools, pool halls, bar rooms or where ever I could go and persuade people to come and hear the Word being preached. ("Revival Meetin's" were the "what's kickin'" thing to do in that day. Nowadays, the perception with most unchurched people is, "now let me make sure I understand, if I go and listen to a guy yelling, stomping, spitting, and screaming, telling me what a sorry "no count" I am, am I to understand it will help me have a better life?")

One afternoon as I was meeting with the pastor of this particular church, making plans to go out and "bring them in," he asked me a question that seemed rather dumb and boring at the time. He asked, "Ron, when are we going to pray?" I said, "Aww, Pastor, we can pray later, let's go out and visit in homes and bring 'em in!" Again, "But Ron, when are we going to pray?" "Pastor, I don't want to pray, I want to go win people to Jesus!"

Finally, with a penetrating look, this precious pastor squared off at me with great love and compassion when he spoke a truth that I have never forgotten. "Ron, little prayer equals little power, much prayer equals much power!" Wow! Since that time, whenever I have lived as if to prove that mighty man of prayer wrong, I have only proved him right![81]

On the baseball field, swinging with a loaded bat is highly illegal due to its unfair advantage of causing the ball, upon impact, to go further than it normally would. In the baseball game of life, however, the "loaded bat" of prayer is not only legal, it is an absolute necessity if we are going to continue stepping up to the plate and making contact with the "baseballs of life" that are thrown our way. If there is the least desire in your heart to be a "power hitter," a regular prayer time is even *more* paramount! Let me ask you, do you have the desire to be a power hitter? If not then either, (a.) right now ask your Heavenly Daddy to give you that desire or, (b.) close this book immediately because great conviction might come upon you!

Since we live in a day in which mega-churches can have five thousand people for a Sunday service or a special event but only fifty when it is time for "prayer meeting," let me, in the words of Ricky Ricardo, "splain Lucy" why this is the case. Unfortunately to so many people, "prayer time" is a boring, spiritual "pshyco-cybernetical" type of time in which a person just goes through all of the "bless 'ems" they can possibly think of. Or it only amounts to a spiritual batting practice that is stumbled through during times of great crisis, in which prayer just kind of seems like the thing to do at the time, hoping that just maybe someone in the "great somewhere who hears every word" might be listening.

"Do ya think" that the reason for the only account that we have in the Gospel accounts of 'da boys who hung with Jesus asking Him to teach them anything is that of "Lord, teach us to pray"[82] is because they observed His prayer time as being like what I just described in the above paragraph? "I don't think so!" If that were me, I would have probably asked something "deeply spiritual" like "Lord, You're pretty good at causing the food dollar to stretch. It was so cool how you made the loaves and fish feed that big crowd. If you wouldn't mind, would you teach me how to bless my food so that one hamburger patty could feed the whole fam? You know Lord that would *really* help with the grocery bill!" Or maybe, "Will You teach me how to heal the sick and raise the dead? This way we could put all of the ambulance chasing attorneys and dishonest doctors out of business!" Although I say this, I am not so sure if I would have asked the frivolous or not. Had I observed, as the eleven out of the twelve did, the prayer life of Jesus, maybe I too would have realized the truth that if I could learn the how, what, when, and where of prayer, I could be all that God has called me to become and therefore do whatever He wanted me to do!

I'm hearing voices again..."I wish that I had that kind of time to pray but I'm just so busy!" Did you know that when it comes to time, however, we all stand on equal ground? Not one single person, or married for that matter, has twenty-six hours in a day. In all my "young" days, I have yet to meet even an older person who has been granted twenty-four and a half hours in a day. One time I tried to talk the Lord into an extension of the twenty-four hour day. He said, "Son, if I gave you Type-A's a twenty-eight hour day, you'd book it for twenty-nine hours!"

It is not by accident that the Gospel accounts of Jesus' earthly ministry show us just how busy He was during those three and half years. In fact there were times that He was so busy that He could not even finish a meal, due to all of the multitudes who needed His attention.[83] Yet it is also very specific as to how busy, busy Jesus took time to pray.[84] The "only begotten Son" of God, Who remember was just as much man as if He were not God and just as much God as if He were not man, still saw the importance of making a prayer time priority! He would spend entire nights in prayer, then come down and heal the sick, raise the dead, and know just what to say to stop the Pharisees dead in their tracks. How many times do we only spend five minutes in prayer and then wonder why we have very little spiritual strength. He knew of the truth that time alone with the Father is to the spirit man (or woman, I'm trying to be a 21st Century kind of guy) what food is to the physical man.

What is the old saying that "an army runs on its stomach!" This is because without the proper nourishment, an army will not have the strength to fight. And so it is with the "GHMC!" (God's Heavenly Marine Corps). Unless this truth gets into our "gut of guts," there will probably always be little or no time for a prayer time. Until we realize that the basic bottom line reason that we continue to get our spiritual rears kicked by the enemy is because we are not dressed for battle,[85] our spiritual rears will continue to be kicked between our shoulders. The old hymn says, "Put on the Gospel armor, each piece put on with prayer..." This is absolutely true. Read Ephesians 6 and you'll see what the pieces of "armor" are of which I speak. Let me reiterate how as United States Marines, we were taught that the reason you do not go out "diddy-bopping" through the jungle of a combat zone in cut-offs and a t-shirt is because you will catch the shrapnel of the enemy. In case you have not realized it yet, we are in the middle of a full scale spiritual war! Satan and the demons of hell are out to destroy everything that we hold near and dear in our families, churches, and this great nation. Everything in those three arenas that is "true, pure, noble, right, and just," the enemy is out to tear down.[86]

Let me ask you a question that you can answer honestly since this is one time that I cannot hear your answer. Are you or are you not experiencing Holy Spirit power in your life? Are you experiencing "much power or little power in your life?" I am not asking if your church services are exciting. (For most Evangelicals, that means people walking the aisle. For some Charismatics, it may mean the number of people jumping pews, falling over and swinging from the closest available chandelier.) Yes, I too have experienced that season of being a spiritual thrill seeker and/or a spiritual exhibitionist. I love a great church service!

Experiencing Holy Spirit power on a daily basis usually will not be in the realm of the magnificent. For most of us, most of the time it will be experienced in the SuperCenter checkout line by *not* giving the check-out clerk a piece of our mind when it takes twenty minutes to get through the line.[87] *Loving our wives as Christ loved the church*[88] will mean not giving them "what for" when we expected a full, hot meal when we got home from work and all she had time to prepare was

"KFC to go." It means, gentlemen, not "shopping for our wives" in the Victoria's Secret's catalogue because our wives have put on a few pounds and the merchandise "scratches an itch."[89] Ladies, it means *respecting your husband*[90] by being sensitive to his needs and moving in the direction of being all that you can be physically. It means being loving and kind to the person at our jobs who has shafted us.[91] (I'm not saying we need to be door mats.) Are you getting my drift?

When we initially come to Christ, over the first few months, it is usually, in retrospect, much easier not to "cuss, smoke or chew, or run with women who do." But then as we grow in the Lord, ouch, that "death to self" stuff really hurts! And the "crucified life" of laying down our attitudes, mindsets, and expectations, "oh man, that's asking a lot!" And you are absolutely right! It does hurt and it does take a lot. However, this is what is known as the crucified life, which is what Christ meant when He said, "If any person wants to follow me, let him deny himself and take up his cross and follow me."[92]

I understand. At times, what I have just written seems so overwhelming to me as well. Some days I live this truth and some days I do not. But the only way that any of us can "take up our cross" and choose death to our own self is by regularly plugging into the Power that is available. It is only as a result of a prayer time in which we are not doing all of the talking but one in which we are listening as much as, if not more than, we are talking that we really plug into Holy Spirit power.[93] In no way am I saying that God does not desire to move in the realm of the spectacular. Holy Spirit power, in its purest form, however, is simply the power to choose the power to do whatever He has called us to be and do.[94] Full realization that we as believers have the power to choose the power to "take up our cross," in any given circumstance, will only come on a consistent basis when we consistently make a dynamic prayer time priority.

As we learn to pray, we will hold a "loaded bat" in our hands as we step up to the home plate of life each day, fully prepared for whatever balls are thrown our way each and every day.

Always know that,

LITTLE PRAYER=LITTLE POWER,
MUCH PRAYER=MUCH POWER

CHAPTER 12

LET'S PLAY BALL!

Principle Number 12: Just Because U-Have the Uniform on Does NOT Mean U-R in the Game!

One of the ministries that I was involved in for the past several years was Contemporary Christian Music Radio. My attire has totally changed from the pastoral suit and tie. In fact you could say *"I've Gone Country!"* Yes, most days you will find my business/"dress" apparel consists of blue jeans, nice shirt with shirt tail out, and cowboy boots. In my early days of ministry, however, I could have been on the cover of the now classic piece of literature, "Dress For Success." How could God bless my preaching unless I wore a three piece suit? Rumors are still floating around that accuse me of always wearing suits to my high school classes. Somehow it was instilled in me that if you dressed sharp and looked like you knew what you were doing, doors would open for you and you would be treated like somebody. I found that to be true. Doors were opened and I was treated like somebody!

As a teenage boy who looked sharp in a suit and tie, I had no trouble whatsoever walking past the guards to meet Dr. Billy Graham and Pat Boone or getting backstage at the

Battle of the Bands to hang out with the "Happy Goodmans." That day of course is "*Gone With the Wind*," in which the term "security" was primarily associated with jail cells, prisons, or the military. At the large public gatherings where it was necessary, security then was not like it is today.

Admittedly I was a rather peculiar teenager, yet I did get to do some activities and meet some people that the average teenage preacher boy does not. Should I have been a kid when it was time to have been a kid? Probably so! One day several years ago, that great "business mogul" and my good friend Bobby Duane, who has been mentioned several times throughout this book, leaned across the table at a Barnes and Noble and said, "Ron, you've lived your life faster than anybody I've ever known!" Please know that although there might be some truth to that statement, I am in no way encouraging nor advocating that everyone should live their life as fast or as close to the edge as I seemingly do. I especially would not want anyone to go over the edge as I have on occasions. However, I am convinced that untold millions of Americans *"dress up but never leave their house"* when it comes to living! They are so afraid to "get out of the boat!" Yes, the Lord did have to rescue Peter from drowning when he started to sink, but he got to "tell his grandkids" of the experience of walking on water![95] (Personally, I think he put the Lord in a rather awkward position. Let's face it, what else was Jesus going to say when asked, "If you are the Lord, tell me to come?" I promise you that even if He would have tried to quickly speak out a, "Yes, it's me but don't jump, I'll be there in a second," Peter would have been already out of the boat by the time He said "Yes, it's me!")

All or nothing, maybe, but as I said, he had the experience of being the only other man to walk on water!

As you have concluded by now, my life has been anything but *boring!* Over the past several years of being somewhat in the spotlight on just a local level, I have experienced how at different times people really get into my life with a "rumor mill" that runs at full throttle! Honestly, there have been times that I have wondered, "Do these people not have a life?!" Between the some truths, half truths, and no truths, I have also wondered if there are really those out there who do not have anything better to do in their day than to wake up and think, "Gee, I wonder what we can come up with on Ron Moore today?!?" Like I said, this is just on a local level. Just think about those who are in the national spotlight! Why do you think the supermarket tabloids and television shows posing as legitimate news shows like *Entertainment Tonight, Access Hollywood,* and the others that I cannot think of, are so successful? Many are so desperate to have a life, they must watch a desperate housewife! This has to be because so many people lead such boring lives that they live to get their excitement vicariously from the lives of other people, whether they are real or not!

Although most people have accepted that life is not a constant "high," this has been a life lesson that I am still learning. There are times in which I consciously have to remind myself that it is okay when a day is not full of the excitement of being in front of people and that everyone has to do grunt work every now and then. Yes, accepting the day to day grind has been a struggle for me since my high school days. As I mentioned earlier, I was radically changed at age fourteen at youth camp and returned home with this huge burden to bring other people to Jesus. As a result of this experience, I was on the radio at fifteen and all during high school was either preaching revival meetings or traveling and being a part of some of the greatest crusades in American history. Exciting!

Sitting in a high school math class trying to figure out what "P" was going to do to "Q" if "R" ran and jumped on it or conjugating sentences, *boring!* After all, the world was "going to hell in a hand basket" and I was stuck in a classroom involved in what seemed like, at the time, trivial pursuits.

Maybe you are a boisterous extrovert who likes to play the game of life like you are up to bat and it is the ninth inning, bases loaded, and all your team needs to win the tournament is for you to make one more good hit. You tend to live by the adage that if it were not for the last minute, nothing would get done! Or maybe you are the introvert who likes to play the game with a steady three point lead who can be counted on for a good base hit. If you have a report due on Friday, you must have it done by Wednesday or you get really hard to live with!

Let me assure you again that while God did not call you to live *my* life, neither did He call you to live a boring life with the main excitement coming from a television or a movie screen! When I write about being in the baseball game of life, I am not writing about just putting on the uniform and spending the majority of your life on the bench watching the other players as they experience the agony and the ecstasy of the game of life. *I'm hearing voices again!* "But Ron, I'm only a carpenter," or "I spend eight hours a day in an office," "I'm a school teacher,"

"I'm only a mom," "I'm just a nurse," or "I sell hospice care to dying people, how exciting can that be?"

The real excitement comes from swinging at three types of pitches. The MOST exciting plays in the day to day game of life are when we are brought to the point of becoming like Jesus, facing our own personal giants and making a difference in individual lives for all of eternity. Throughout this book, I have attempted to open up some of the good, the bad, and the ugly of my life, all of which is laced with redemption, repentance, and the mind boggling mercy and grace of God. After over thirty-nine years, when most people my age are at least starting to unwind and gear towards retirement, I am just warming up! The excitement of becoming like Jesus a little more everyday, facing my personal giants and making a difference in lives is what keeps *me* in this game, and I know these three challenges can do the same for *you!*

Earlier in this chapter I mentioned how so many times we put on the uniform for the game but do not get involved in the game. As you read this book, maybe you feel as though your job, marriage, the education process you are currently in, or maybe just life in general is boring! If that is the case, it is time to get off of the bench and get in the game! As you get in the game of becoming like Christ, you will discover that there is no higher or more exciting goal to strive for. You must understand that this goal will never be fully accomplished until we see Him face to face.[96]

One huge part of this process of becoming like Christ is the exciting challenge of facing our very own personal giants. Getting *dressed up but never leaving the house* (so to speak) is nothing new. I Samuel 17 tells of how each day for forty days, the Israeli Army got dressed in battle array, then just stood there and did nothing but shake in their boots when a giant named Goliath came out. Goliath had not even attacked them physically, he only launched verbal rockets against them. You know the story of how "only a boy named David" came onto the scene and changed the course of history. The truth is every one of us have giants in our lives. Some of our giants may be known by friends and family. Others of us may have giants that only we and our Heavenly Daddy know about. It does not matter whether or not your giant is publicly acceptable or one that embarrasses you and the entire family. Although twenty first century giants are not seen with the naked eye, nor fought with weapons used with our hands, they are just as real, big, and intimidating to us as Goliath was to those Israeli troops of that day.

Definition: a 21st Century giant may be a person, place, or thing that, whenever your paths cross, usually your walk in the Spirit turns into a walk in the flesh.

Whether your giant is the lust of the flesh, the pride of life, an open bottle of alcohol, an open refrigerator door, lying, a critical/gossipy tongue, unforgiveness, prayerlessness, an unbelieving heart, cheating on a test in school, cheating on a business deal, letting your thoughts run wild, depression, or whatever it is that challenges the control of Jesus Christ in your life, you have a giant to contend with! And that is all right! Having a giant does not mean that you are not right with the Lord. If you recognize that you have them, this is the first step in the process of conquering them. And one of the exciting things about giants is that when we conquer one, the Lord has a way of showing us another one that still needs to be conquered. Remember, I am not referring to the everyday, run of the mill sin. You leave the office late and drive twenty miles over the speed limit trying to be on time. Or the boss chews you out and you go home and kick the dog, yell at the kids, and are cranky towards your spouse that night. We are always going to have days like that from time to time, or at least until our children slap us in a Rest Home. Rather, I am referring to those "repeat sins" that we have struggled with, felt guilty over, and said that we would never, never do again, until the next time![97] The kind of sin that we know better, yet we do it anyway and then feel like such a schmuck towards God.

Let us look at "only a boy named David" and how he conquered Goliath. There are some principles found in 1 Samuel 17 that we can apply to our giants. The first action David took was in his mind. When everyone else was shaking in their boots saying it could not be done, he recognized Goliath for who he really was. In fact he went into "math mode" (golly I hate to admit that) and made an equation. He said to himself: Uncircumcised Philistine vs. Army of the Living God = Defeat for Uncircumcised Philistine. He did not see Goliath as this giant ogre, he saw him as an uncircumcised Philistine whose size did not make any difference because he knew that he was nowhere near as big as Almighty God! This was not because of "the power of positive thinking." He knew this because the powerful positive Word of God told the *Kids of Israel* that they were to take the land and wipe out all the residue of Philistines.[98]

Okay, it is time once again for reader participation. It is time to "fess up" to the fact that you have a giant and exactly what or who that giant is. *Let's play ball!* Right now I am going to ask you to bring up on the computer screen of your mind who or what it is that brings you down and keeps you from making contact with the ball when you get up to the plate. Let me remind you, I am talking about the people, situations, or circumstances that even after spending that *Sweet Hour of Prayer*" and Bible study, when confronted with (fill in the blank) more times than not, you have found yourself swinging at the devil's curve ball. Now that you have this in mind, I want you to make the same equation that young David did when confronting Goliath. "Uncircumcised Philistine" of ____ _____ vs. the Lord Jesus who lives in me = defeat for _____!99

Now you are dressed for battle. But between now and the time you actually come face to face with this giant, remember the faithfulness of God. As you gain strength from receiving God's Word into your life, look back on the times that He has come through for you. Even if all you can think of is the fact that you woke up today on this side of the dirt, begin to praise and thank Him for life. David told King Saul who tried to discourage him, "Hey, God helped me defend my sheep from a lion and a bear, and the same God who was bigger than the lion and bear is bigger than this giant of an uncircumcised Philistine!" (RMRV).

Realize that while the playing field or the circumstances may have changed, the size and strength of your God has not and will not change!100 That fateful summer I turned fourteen, I was working at (something else that is virtually *Gone With the Wind*) a service station. Yeah, looking back I cannot believe how many times as a "not quite fourteen" year old boy I was left alone to run a ten pump service station. (Ooh, in this crazy age we live in, maybe I could find the owner and sue him for taking advantage of an underage worker?) Often times I would have a car up on the rack and in the process of changing the oil when other cars would drive up needing (Yet another blast from the past) 25 cent per gallon gasoline. One particular make and model of car had a plug to its oil pan in which I had a real struggle in getting back on. I am not sure why, but this particular car just gave me fits. I will never forget how one time, with several cars having just pulled up to the pumps and trying to screw the plug back in this challenging type of car, I stopped and asked the Lord to help me get the plug put back in and guess what, He did! It went in the very next time.

How many times I have referred back to that instance, knowing that if the Lord could help me with that, He could help me with whatever was confronting me. And what a great feeling it is when you let that curve ball fly by knowing that while it looked good, you wanted to swing at it, would have felt good at the time to have swung but, by the grace of God and the power of the Holy Spirit in your life, you did not swing at it!

Although it was exciting being on the road and doing what I had the privilege of doing during my teenage years, one of the negatives was that I did not have to learn how to work out differences with people. After all, if you did not get along with a particular pastor or church staff member, hey, after the meeting was over, I was moving on down the road. As I touched on in Chapter 1, the mindset was that of "when the going gets tough, the tough get going, on down the road." Earlier I talked about being fired from a mega church staff for the *deeply spiritual* reason of not meeting quota of the number of families that were supposed to join the church each week. It turned out to be a really neat experience, as we actually stayed the course and finished the time God had for us at that church. Although we wanted to run and attend another church, we did not! While I had been released from the full time church staff, I had not been released from the ministry of that church. No, we were right back in the congregation the very next Sunday. Over the next year and a half of being faithful, the Lord turned our relationship with that pastor around and when it was time for us to go and start the church in Denver, they blessed us and sent us out with a chunk of change to help start the new work. But it was not until we were loading the U-Haul that it really hit me. I looked at my wife and said, "Ya know, for the first time, we've finished the course. We didn't cut and run when the going got tough!" And did it feel good to know that!

Victory begets victory! Once you have experienced Holy Spirit power over your giant, it will be a little bit easier the next time it shows up to fall at the feet of Jesus saying, "Lord, I know you are greater in me than this (fill in the blank), please help me again to allow you to be or do what I cannot be or do without your strength." The Biblical account of Goliath the Second makes this clear. In II Samuel 21, we are told of how several giants had once again come up against the Israeli Army, some years after Goliath the First had fallen from the stone flung by a teenage David. One of the giants mentioned in this chapter is the second time in which we see the name "Goliath" appear. However this time, they did not hurl verbal spears at one another for forty days. They did not bite their fingernails in fear as to what in the world they were going to do. This time, when "Big G II" appeared, the scripture records how they just killed him. No muss, no fuss. Because of what David had done years before, they knew that the "Big G" was "goin' down."

It is hard to describe the satisfaction that comes from taking care of whatever your "Big G II" might be. For me it was one night, nearly eight months into the experience of which I wrote in Chapter 9. Without a shred of any evidence as to the accusations leveled against me, the woman whom I knew I would grow old with had not only left but the divorce of which she filed for was almost legally final and there was no change of her heart in sight. To help you appreciate the account of the night of which I am about to share with you, I must first confess that I do not play "Uno" very well. During this time however, and rightfully so, I did virtually everything, outside of the public ministry, alone. My friends were all married and I certainly was not single. I especially hate eating alone! I fully believe the scripture is absolutely right when it says that it "is not good for man (especially this man) to be alone." Now that I have allowed you into my constitution a "skosh bit" more, maybe you can appreciate the account I am about to tell you of the night I personally encountered "Big G II" face to face.

It was one of those extra tough nights in which, although I did not want to be alone, I knew that I had to be. After "much thought" it was decided! The fastest relief in sight was to stop in to the neighborhood Blockbuster and pick up a video. As I got out of my car a very attractive college girl, whom I had met while she worked the cash register at a small local retail store, met me as I was going in. You must understand however, this was not just any attractive college girl of whom I had made her acquaintance. Our acquaintance was made because when I was checking out at her cash register, upon recognizing the name on my debit card, excitement gripped her very being and stars filled her eyes. "Oh my gosh, you're Ron Moore!" She had to call some friends and tell them that "Ron Moore" had been in her store. And by this particular night, I had done business a couple more times in her store. Each time, the stars in her eyes got bigger. So between her starry eyes and my loneliness, it should not be a shocker that when she was exiting the Blockbuster as I was entering, sparks flew! Having the gift of gab is at times a curse. As we stood there talking for what was only a brief time, she informed me how she was going to have to be alone herself that night watching the video she had rented. Instantly, the enemy whispered in my ear, "You don't have to be alone tonight. You could be with her! You could be with a college girl tonight! All you have to do is come back with a 'well there's no need for both of us to be alone, how about some company?'" The old Ron Moore would have jumped at that opportunity. But that night, just as clearly as I heard the voice of the enemy, *The Voice of Truth* spoke louder as He said, "Flee youthful lusts!"[101] I quickly ended the conversation and walked in the video store literally shaking. In case you do not know, when a guy my age turns down an evening with an attractive college girl who already has stars in her eyes, the ego screams, "Are you crazy?!" After only a couple of minutes of looking and seeing nothing but the kind of movies that I did not need to watch, I quickly left. Not fifty yards away from the Blockbuster, once again the voice of the Holy Spirit spoke to me saying, "You just killed your second Goliath," and did it feel great knowing that I had been obedient and did the will of my Heavenly Daddy.

In no way am I saying that you will never again swing at that same curve ball, however, you will at least know that you know that you "can do all things through Christ who gives you strength!"[102] Never give up! Some giants take longer to die than others. Remember part of the excitement of becoming like Jesus is in doing battle with your giants. Are you really doing battle with your giants, or are you simply going through the motions of playing church and dressing for the game but never really doing battle?

Finally (I know, that sounds so preachery), you have set your "eyes on the prize of the high calling" to become like Christ and step up to the plate although you are afraid of striking out. Yes, you are to be commended for not swinging at the same types of curve balls formerly swung at. Now, it is also time to make a difference in lives. What I am about to suggest does not include, unless God specifically tells you to, going up to complete strangers in airports and careening down the Romans Road while they listen. At whatever place you happen to be in your process of becoming like Christ, you can make a positive difference in lives! Combine the feeling of knowing that you and Jesus have slain one of your personal giants with knowing that God has used you to touch someone's life with His love and you have a huge "WOW" kind of life.

When the kids were all in grade school, some of the most memorable times were when we would go buy groceries for some family whom we knew was going through tough financial times. After we bought the groceries, we would then drive to their neighborhood and park down the block, out of sight.

Then, just as it was getting dark, we would sneak up to their front door, set the bags of food and supplies down, ring the door bell and run and hide. Most of those folks never knew who it was, but boy were we blessed in knowing we had made a difference! The fact is that God has uniquely made you and gifted you to be an extension of His love in ways that nobody else but you can be.[103] You have the ability to see needs and meet those needs that absolutely no one else can, simply because no one else has walked quite the exact road that you have.

Maybe you are a "mercy person" who can go up to a co-worker and say, "I'm sorry you're going through what you're going through, and this may sound crazy but I just want you to know that I am praying for you." Or your middle name may be "Organization." You could go and help a "messy" learn how to organize their house and thus help in restoring order to their life. Recently, I had the opportunity to do some voice work for a couple of college kids who were working on an animated film project for a class. The original script had several curse words. I told my agent that I would not do it with those in it. She inadvertently told them that I was a preacher, not that I'm ashamed, it is just when people hear that, they tend to expect you to either be a certain way or "whip a witness" on them, so they changed the script. As I was there that evening doing the work, I had such a good rapport with them that I thought as I left, "you know, when these boys want to talk about spiritual matters, I just bet they'll give me a call." Not because I went there rebuking the demons of foul language, broke all of the liquor bottles they proudly had lined up on the shelf, or had an air about me that communicated that they were so privileged to have *me* come and help with their unholy project. No, I genuinely believe those who have not really experienced the Lord need to see real people who really do experience Him in whatever crazy situation "life happens" in.

Let me ask you again…are you ready to get in the ball game? The choice is yours. Put the uniform on and sit on the bench of a boring life *or* accept God's calling of playing in the game, becoming like Christ, slaying some giants along the way and making a difference throughout all eternity in the lives of the people whom God gives you to touch with His love. You, my friend, have been given everything you need to be as well as to do what He has called you to, if you have genuinely received the New Birth in Christ![105]

Go Ahead…It's UR Day & UR Turn Up 2 Bat

CHAPTER 13

IF YOU'RE STILL READING THIS, YOU'RE STILL IN THE GAME

Principle Number 13: For Each Day We're Giv-N, We're Giv-N His Grace 2 Keep Moving On

It is totally blowing my mind that as I conclude this book, I have over thirty-nine years of ministry behind me. (Remember, I started at a very young age, thank-you!) However, from time to time it feels good to be able to look at certain trends, fads, and flairs that have taken place amongst the "church set" through the looking glass of years of experience. "Frinstance" we dressed up, now we dress down. Some churches look at you strange if you wear blue jeans, while some of those who want "freedom" to wear the clothes that are "you" look at "you" real strange if "you" happen to have a suit and tie on. Another observation is how, if I did not know better, I would think certain truths and scriptures were just recently added to the Bible. Around ten years ago, I think the Lord surely must have just slipped Jeremiah 29:11 in because all you heard everywhere you turned was how God had "plans for good and not for evil" in our lives. Then we discovered that because Jabez asked God to bless him, we can too! Somebody *Kissed Dating Goodbye*, so therefore anyone who happens to go out on a date with someone of the opposite sex whom they have not somehow already determined that they want to marry is just flat out of the will of God! And to top everything, in many circles the "Builder Generation" is fighting "tooth and toenail" with the "Baby Boomers" over keeping the hymnals in the backs of the pews. While in other circles (and this really boggles my mind), the Boomers are fighting with the Gen X'ers over not singing the same choruses that we broke away from the hymnals to sing in the late '70's through the early '90's!

Please know that I am in no way badmouthing believing that God's plans for you are good (I mentioned that truth a couple of times in this book) or that you can ask Him to bless you. And if the Lord has told you not to date, then "by dingy" you better eat your meals alone and wait for "Mister" or "Miss Right" to show up at your door step. (Which if you live by this rule, you really should look presentable and set an extra plate.) All I am saying is that it is amusing to have watched the different trends of "Christianity" that "mushroom" and are seemingly everywhere you turn for a while, then you seldom hear of them anymore.

One of the scriptures that was "added" somewhere around the late '60's was John 10:10, "…But I have come that they might have life and have it more abundantly." For about eight to ten years this verse about the "abundant life" that Christ came to give was seemingly the only verse anyone quoted. Although I am certain that youth leaders and evangelists, along with all of the BTE's, of the day never intended for *stinkin' thinkin'* to set in but because of the high usage of this verse, somehow it did.

At least with so many of us, the mindset of hearing about *"the abundant life, the abundant life"* was that as long as we pushed the right spiritual buttons and Jesus was Lord, then everything would "come up roses" because after all, we are promised the abundant life!

Obviously our definition as to what the abundant life consists of is not exactly accurate, to say the least. On occasion it seems as if those who make no claims at striving to serve our Lord have a better handle on the big picture of life than do we. (Whoa, get ready, I'm having another rare moment of appreciating my age again!) One of the truths that has taken many years to learn is that from start to finish, depending on how many years we wake up on this planet, is that life is made up of numerous "ups, downs, and all arounds!" And through all of them, the abundant life is to be lived in the middle of all of the seasons and challenges of life simply because of the abundance of God's grace that produces a joy and peace that defies all reasoning.[102]

After fifteen or sixteen years of going to practice and practice games, most of us actually step up to the plate of life during high school or college. The majority of us get a firm grip on the bat and although it may take a few tries, we usually get a base hit. First Base: *"It's all good!"* Although we are aware that there are still two more bases to touch before we go home, we are excited that we are actually on our way! Yes, we are aware, at least mentally, that there are players on the other team who are just waiting for the opportunity to throw us out, but we are pumped about the potential of going all the way home and making the score.

Have you ever known someone, or maybe you've done

this yourself, who has tried to live life on the adrenaline rush of the hit and the ensuing run to that very first base? Maybe they have decided to just stay and try to live the remainder of their life on first base. After all, it is exciting and the possibility exists that they could get thrown out on their way to or at second! Although the thought of stealing second base is really exciting, they have never done it before and after all, they did make it to first! A person's temperament will have a huge effect on whether their struggle is that of wanting to live on the excitement of first base or the fear of running to second.

Unfortunately, it is no longer just the Hollywood crowd who feels like after the "goose pimples of the relationship" stage is gone, it must mean that love is no longer. With at least fifty years of the glorification of "young love" in the movies, our culture leans this way far too often. Although it is hard to imagine our culture ever being this way, I remember my momma telling of a time in which people who were ages thirteen through nineteen, were just ages thirteen through nineteen. There was no subculture of *"The teenager-er-er-er!"* Yes, I personally believe that God's design for the teenage years is for that season to be the most carefree and fun season of our life. Along with learning, growing into a new stage, and testing our wings, it is basically to be carefree and fun. But sooner or later we all have to move on. We have to buy our own groceries, pay our own bills, make our own tough decisions, and deal with the struggles of our own marriage. Looking back, I only thought I had a heartache when Mary Ann turned down my offer to give her a ride home from school and because of that, I had my first car wreck. (Well actually it was because I was singin' da' blues along with Johnny Rivers, only I changed the words from *Baby I Need Your Lovin'* to Mary, I need your lovin', and as I was crooning, looking off to the blue sky, surprise, surprise, the car in front of me stopped! It was only a four-car collision with no injuries though. Thankfully the car behind me rear ended my car as well.)

Hopefully you can look back at those years and what at the time seemed challenging and say, "it was a cake walk" compared to the real world of adult life. Tragically, for many people life has gotten so complicated or, even more tragically, so boring that mentally, we longingly return to those days far too often. Have you ever encountered an old classmate who when you talk to them, it is as if they have never gotten out of high school? While most people do not take it to that extreme, far too many people go back mentally to high school or college days of the past in order to relieve the hurt and pain of the present.

No doubt, our first real hit that we make as a young adult is a feeling of ecstasy! With our friends and family yelling "You da' man" or "You go, girlfriend," there is nothing quite like that "first kiss" feeling. Whether it is high school or college graduation, new love, new marriage, new baby, or landing the job you really want and getting your first raise, the feeling of "new" is grand! You got your first hit while up at life's plate and you made it to first base. The feeling is second to none. Fortunately however, in the big scheme of our lives, tomorrow is a new day. Certainly we need to appreciate the good and learn from the challenges of yesterday, but today is the only day that we have for sure. If we try to live in yesterday's successes we will surely fail to live in the promises for success that God has for us today. No, you may not even make what you think is a base hit today, but if you are in the game and can lay your head on your pillow knowing that you have accomplished everything your Heavenly Daddy set forth for you to accomplish this day, then you are a success today. Jesus had the most precise definition of success. Shortly before His death, He was able to say, "I have accomplished all that the Father had for me to accomplish."[106] That, my friend, is true success! But in order to accomplish all that God has for us to accomplish by the end of our life, we have to accomplish it one day at a time![107]

Can you imagine Barry Bonds, showing up at his next baseball game with the San Francisco Giants, saying, "You know boys, I got a homerun during our last game, I don't think I'll step up to the plate today. What if I struck out? That would be real embarrassing so if it's all the same to you, I think I'm going to sit on the bench and think about that homerun I made during our last game." (Of course, first off, the owner would have a little chat with him as to the fact that he's not paying him the astronomical salary he's paying him to sit on the bench.) Not only would he disappoint his team as well as the fans, but it would not be very long at all until the excitement of the game was completely absent from his life! Barry Bonds the homerun hitter would become Barry Bonds the rut waiting to happen! I once heard it said that a rut is nothing but a "grave with the ends kicked out." Are you in a rut?

As ludicrous as that example is, so many people live their lives in a rut, holding on to the "hits" they made in the past. Let me reiterate that, while we need to learn from past challenges and hold near to our hearts great victories, we serve a God whose name is "I AM,"[108] not "I WAS!" A few years ago,

Carolyn Arends sang a hit song rightly titled "Seize the Day." One of the main lines in this great song is, "Seize the day, for life slips away just like hour glass sand, seize the day…" Unless we make the choice to rejoice in each day we are given, we not only miss all that God has for us in everyday life, but we will most certainly find ourselves in a rut, enduring life rather than enjoying it.[109]

Second Base: By the time most of us touch second, we have fully realized that there really are nine other players from the opposite team who are ready, willing, able, and just looking for the opportunity to throw us out. Although there are a few people who "steal second" and arrive early, it takes most of us a little longer. Because of the realization of all of the dangers and how easily we could have gotten out, there are those of us who although obviously have chosen to move on from first, decide that moving on to third base and risking an "out" is just too big of a risk, therefore we choose to live on second base the remainder of our lives. After all, we are not living in the "Glory Days" of our "first" base hit. "No sir-ree-bobby," we have gone on to second! But is it ever tough, with bills piling up and child rearing hassles that never seem to stop. Trying to survive a marriage and pleasing a boss. Or maybe your marriage did not survive or you have lost your job. If you have experienced health problems, no doubt pain and physical discomfort can obviously challenge your quality of life. With everything that is going on in your life, time for yourself may be something you are envisioning as not happening until you arrive at the "rest home." If you are a single parent, a "date" might be something you only see in the produce aisle of the grocery store. Unexpected turns of events, in whatever form, can absolutely take their toll on our very being. Some people struggle for years with the fact that their life or the family life that they envisioned as a child did not turn out like they always thought that it would.

Have you experienced so many tough times that you catch yourself buying in to the philosophy of "life's hard then you die?" Does the thought of running to third base "scare the pants off" of you? Is a dream something you only have at night while you are sleeping, and many of those are bad ones? You are not alone by any means. Probably most people, when they make their first hit, have dreams of scoring big as they make it to first base. However, by the time most of us have reached second, life happens in numerous, unexpected ways in which although our "momma said, there'd be days like this," she just did not tell us there would be so many! Consequently, as we are trying so desperately to keep our heads above water and some semblance of sanity, we find ourselves much too overwhelmed with the happenings of our life thus far and/or we are just flat scared to death to try whatever it would take to get off of our comfort zone of standing safe on second base and make a run for third.

My observation has been that the number of movers, shakers, and dreamers begins thinning out by age twenty-five. By thirty-five, the numbers dwindle even more. And by forty-five, a common school of thought is that if you have not achieved success and happiness by now...you won't! If living on second base even "kind-a-sorta" describes you, please do not up and quit your job or leave your marriage. I believe it was Dr. Jimmy Draper who said, "God may not always deliver you out of the fire. Sometimes He delivers you in the fire."[110] But one way or the other, He will deliver you!" You can make a run to third base! God says that you "can do all things through Christ who gives you strength."[111] It may sound trite but it is a "reality statement" that He can "make a way where there seems to be no way."[112] Since you probably did not arrive at the "scared to death to make a run for it state of mind" overnight, it is safe to say that neither will you get out of it overnight. But you can regain your strength and courage and make a successful run to third base! Being able to "do *all things* through Christ" can only mean that you can do everything that He wants you to do. Ask yourself, or even better yet, ask the Lord, "Do You want me to stay on second base, caught up in all of the happenings of life? Is this all I was created for, to have a good start and then get stuck in the sands of the blahs of life?"

Throughout this book I have tried to be honest about some of the mountaintops as well as the valleys of my life and the truths that have kept me *swinging* in this baseball game called life. I will even confess that I am still learning to live much of what I have already learned. Assuming, which is always dangerous, that you have read all of the book thus far, you know that I have had those seasons of being on second base and feeling trapped, scared, and feeling like there is no way of escape. If you feel this way today, another truth that I have learned that I alluded to in Chapter 9 was that of praise. Remember, there is nothing wrong with being in a huge jam, in and of itself. The jam, whether deserved or undeserved, is most likely the result of one of life's happenings, good, bad, or otherwise. Since you probably cannot instantly change the circumstances that you are in overnight, you must start with changing you. If you will begin to praise the Lord for who He is and His sovereignty in your life, then and only then will you begin to comprehend the incomprehensible size of God. I am talking getting "off the wall" with your praise. Something like, "Lord I thank you that you knew what You were doing when You placed me in the family in which you placed me." Or maybe you need to thank Him that He placed you with the foster parents whom He placed you with. "Lord, I thank You that You were in control when the neighborhood bullies put me down in the manhole that afternoon." (This actually happened to me.) So I can thank God that I have a big sister who rescued me! "Lord, I praise You that even when I took matters into my own hands and made a mess of my life, You saw the big picture of my life and never let me out of Your hands." Do you catch what is going on here? I am not praising the Lord for the bad things that took place. I would never ask you to do that. What we are doing is thanking and praising Him that He has been Lord and in control right in the middle of the good, the bad, and the crazy of our lives![113]

I can promise you with a money back guarantee that as you begin to do this type of extreme praise, your eyes will be taken off of how big of a mess you may have legitimately made of your life or how trapped you may be due to the happenings of life, and you will begin to have a focus on just how big our God is and the fact that truly there is *nothing* too difficult for Him! You will be the one who rapidly changes and you will be just like the three teenage Hebrew boys who were thrown into the fire and experienced deliverance in the fire simply because Jesus went into and through the fire with them.[114] Is that not cool to know that Jesus will go through the fire with you?

Secondly, I can also promise you that while your circumstances and the players may be somewhat unique to you and your situation, you are definitely not the only one who has spent what may seem like most of a season on second base. There are those people who have basically been through what you are currently going through (key word through) who love you and can be your third base coach, giving you proven practical steps as to how to get your second wind and when to make a run for third.[115] Deborah Shelton, who is a single mom, found herself in debt up to her neck and was not making the "big bucks" to quickly change her situation. Instead of moping around having a pity party about being a single mom, she attended a Dave Ramsey *Financial Peace University*. Dave Ramsey is not just a theoretician. At one time he too was in a financial mess to the tune of four million dollars and filed bankruptcy when he was only thirty years old. He decided not to *sing da' blues* the rest of his life. Instead, he sought wisdom as to how to get out of the mess that he had made and because Dave Ramsey came through it, he is now able to help millions of people who are in financial messes as well. Therefore, Ms Shelton is now out of debt and has money in the bank, all without waiting until her "ship came in" for a job that paid the big bucks.

Whatever your situation is, after you have learned to praise Him that He is Lord in all of the circumstances of your life, diligently search for someone who has at least basically been through what you are experiencing who will have some practical steps and can help coach you as to how and when to make a run for third base!

Third Base: Do you feel exhausted, like you came this far and just do not have the energy to even think about running for home? It is so unfortunate that so many people hit the ripe young age of fifty feeling so old. As I mentioned earlier, my wonderful daddy was older when I entered the "fam." By the time he was fifty-five years old he owed no man a thin dime and had a residual income. Not bad for a man who started his adult life as a cotton picker with a sixth grade education. As I also mentioned, I come from a long line of "bull headed" people. My momma and daddy both fit into this category so I did not get this way on my own! So without being mentored or attending a Dave Ramsey course on finances, my daddy went through numerous jobs and entrepreneurial ventures, hitting his head against "God only knows" how many brick walls until he finally succeeded. Daddy definitely instilled in all four of us a work ethic that has also been handed down to my children. This is why a couple of years ago when my son David called saying, "Dad, I want to go into business for myself, I'd like you to look over my business plan," I chuckled and said, "It's in your blood, boy!"

There is something however, that I am trying to avoid, that I saw in my daddy during his later years. While it was a good thing that he experienced the financial success and freedom that he did, by the time he arrived in his early sixties, he was worn out. Had our hard charging choleric momma not, as Daddy used to say, "gotten that sharp stick out" and poked him with it, he would have just sat in his Lazy-Boy and never left the house. I think Daddy's mental and emotional exhaustion is why one of his favorite phrases during those latter years of his life was, "I've done my due!" He lost interest in fishing, gardening, and travel; plus the healthy pressure to get up each morning and live was not there.

Maybe you feel pretty good about making it to third base. You are to be congratulated! You did not remain on second base when the going got tough. And you are pretty satisfied with the way things are in your life. After all, it takes a lot of hard work to get to third base. Whether you have had a successful first, second, or third marriage, your children are grown and your finances set, it has taken all the help the good Lord could give you to get to where you are at this stage of your life. *Hello, Ron, knock-knock, is anybody home?* After all of this, why in heavens name would I want to choose to climb another mountain or cross another ocean? I didn't have a choice, so to speak, with all of the other challenges I've faced in the past! (I think I just heard a small amount of angered frustration in your voice that time.)

One reason and one principle alone will answer that question. Because as long as God gives us breath to breathe, there is someone whom you can touch with His love and encouragement because of what you have come through in life. Plus the fact that life is to be celebrated each day as long as we live here on this planet.[116] Oh I do not mean you should place your entire financial stability in jeopardy or sell out and sail around the world. But at the same time, please do not sit back and say, "I've done my due," and not fulfill the calling that is on your life. Yes, you read that statement correctly. You still have a calling on your life! What are you interested in that even if it took some effort, you could do? Each morning wake up with a grateful heart for another opportunity to "get it right." If you are not by nature creative, ask God to show you ways in which you can make a difference. Whether it is going on mission trips or mentoring younger couples, what a great ministry either of these would be. Sharing with younger couples the fact that there were times you wanted to quit but you didn't, and how you are so glad that you didn't. Or even if your challenge is to invest in the lives of your grandchildren, you can make a difference in somebody's life.

A few different times in this book I have talked about hitting a homerun. In no way am I trying to be like the parent who gets bent out of shape at a child who has worked hard and made an honest effort and still only brings home "B's" and "C's." If you consider yourself to be a player who consistently makes base hits and drives in other players to score, you are still making a difference in the unique way God has made you. Even if there is no record on audio or video tape or a written account of what you have done, you must know that your heavenly Daddy has recorded it all and He says that He is not ashamed to be called your Father.[117] Remember, He is not too concerned with the amount of ability He has given you, but what you do with what has been given you.

The only historical account that haunts me is that of the three leading generals of the 20th Century. Arguably, General Douglas MacArthur and General George Patton were the two greatest battlefield generals of that era. However, both were relieved of their command. Their talent and ability fell subservient to their inability to obey orders. The same chain of command that applies to the private is also applicable to the general. Although most people thirty-five and up would recognize the names of MacArthur and Patton and identify them with World War II, few could tell you the name of one of the other Generals who did not come close to the notoriety or colorful characters of MacArthur and Patton, yet General Omar Bradley was known as the "the soldier's general." Although there was never a major motion picture with him as the leading character, history tells us that he was a good, faithful, and loyal soldier not only throughout his forty-four years of military service, but until the end of his life here on earth in April of 1981. Will Lang Jr. of Life Magazine said, "The thing I most admire about Omar Bradley is his gentleness. He was never known to issue an order to anybody of any rank without first saying, "Please?"

While Generals MacArthur and Patton are without a doubt men to be admired and studied, my heroes have come to be the "General Bradleys" who make it over the long haul of life with a bounce in their mental and emotional step. Women like Sylvia Powers, Coreen Connolly, and Ann Cameron. For years I referred to them as my "three girl friends on the Western Slope of Colorado." They were affectionately known to preachers far and near and to the hundreds of people who knew and lived around them as "The Sisters." These precious ladies were "90's kind of women in the '20's" who never bore children. All three sisters had left their daddy's ranch in Delta, Colorado to pursue their dreams in Hollywood in the 1920's. All three were also part of the "party crowd" of that day. Ann and Coreen came to Jesus first. But after Sylvia's husband died while she was on a trip back to the ranch, she went off the deep end and in her own words had the "bent elbow disease." She began to "party hardy" to drown her sorrows. She was barely into her early forties when "life happened." After awhile her sisters prevailed and brought her to church with them, and she was radically changed by trusting in God's love for her life. "Miss Sylvia," as we called her, went on to become

John McArthur Sr.'s secretary. These giants for God, while unknown by most of the world, were the kind of people in which if you needed someone to pray for you, especially if you were experiencing crisis, you did whatever you could to make contact with them because you knew they knew how to get in touch with God. Yes, everyone who met them was either touched by heaven THROUGH them or they touched heaven FOR them. They were prayer warriors. And what a zest for life they had. When they were ages 85, 88, and 92, they decided they were going "on vacation" up to Wyoming for a few days. I received a post card about a week later explaining how they would not be back at church as scheduled, as they had decided to go on to Canada! They also mentioned on that same card about how a couple of guys had been flirting with Coreen. Oh yes, and you could bet Coreen was flirting back! Real women who had reality with God! A phone call just a few weeks ago confirmed that Miss Ann, at 104 years old, still has her right mind, so I am certain she is still praying for me. Miss Sylvia and Miss Coreen are no doubt interceding for me and many others now that they have made it home and stand before Him face to face. These are just three of the people, the type of which make it over the long haul with no great fanfare, yet with a determination to daily step up to the plate, place a firm grip on the bat and swing at balls that are thrown that they believe they can hit, as long as they awaken in this life.

When you hear the heavenly third base coach signal you to make a run for home, you will run home with all of the energy and strength that the God who spoke the universe into existence can give you.[118] Then you can stand before Him with the confidence of knowing that although you made some hits, took some hits, struck out, and were on the bench for what seemed to be extended periods of time, you continued to step up to the plate and kept on swinging until you made it home and heard "Well done!"[119]

U CAN Finish UR Race that U Were Created 2 Run

ADDENDUM

If after reading the account of many of the C-R-A-Z-Y times of my life you have realized that you really do not have that *personal relationship* with the same Jesus who has loved me unconditionally, never let go nor given up on me and still has a plan for me to win, yes, even after all that I have done. You may be having thoughts like, "Ya know I think I'd like to get to know a God like this." Fasten your seatbelts, because you can! Yes, right where you sit or may be standing, you can experience His unconditional love and complete forgiveness no matter what you have done or how bad the dirty deed that you did. God's love for you is still just as strong as it was when you were only two seconds out of your mother's womb. If you genuinely want to be forgiven and personally meet the Almighty God who created the universe by allowing Him to be the Boss, the Manager, and the CEO of your life, will you pray this simple prayer? *"Dear Jesus, I've really blown it. I've sinned against You. I believe that You died to pay the price in full for all of my past, present, and future sin. Right now, I ask You to forgive me and take total control of my life? Be the Boss of my life from this point on? I ask this in Jesus name, Amen!"*

If you just did this, according to God's Word in Romans 10:13, you are now what is referred to as "saved," because you did what God's Word told you to do. You called on the name of the Lord. On top of what I have written in this book that will help you in "stepping up to the plate" in your new life, find a local church where the Bible is taught as the infallible Word of God, a church that ministers to you, as well as a church that you can be excited about and recommend to your friends.

ENDNOTES

1. Isaiah 43:1&2
2. Psalm 106:12
3. Genesis 9:21
4. Genesis 12:13 & 20:2
5. Genesis 27
6. Exodus 2:11–14
7. II Samuel 11:1–24
8. Hebrews 12:2
9. Romans 8:11
10. Mark 10:9
11. Jeremiah 32:17&27
12. John 8:1–11
13. II Corinthians 5:17
14. Romans 12:1
15. Romans 8:16
16. II Corinthians 5:21
17. Romans 8:17
18. II Cor. 13:4 & Heb. 7:25

19. Ephesians uses this term 90 times
20. Colossians 2:10
21. Galatians 2:16&17
22. Hebrews 7:25
23. Romans 8:29
24. Hebrews 4:15
25. Hebrews 11:16
26. Jeremiah 29:11
27. Romans 12:1
28. Philippians 3:13&14
29. I Corinthians 9:26&27
30. Psalm 37:23
31. Matthew 10:24
32. John 10:10
33. I John 3:1&3; Galatians 5; I John 5:19
34. Isaiah 43:1&2; Romans 8:29
35. Psalm 84:11
36. Philippians 2:12
37. I Peter 1:16
38. Romans 6
39. Hebrews 5:8
40. John 12:23–28&16:7
41. Numbers 13 tells us of the trip only taken approx. 2–2 1/2 years rather than 40.
42. Exodus 23:29&30
43. BIBLE PRINCIPLE: A Bible truth that may or may not be specifically written out, yet the truth of it is seen throughout scripture.
44. Mark 9:44–46
45. Romans 8:37

46. II Corinthians 10:7b
47. II Corinthians 10:5
48. Ephesians 6:10–16
49. Jeremiah 32:27
50. Matthew 9:29
51. Hebrews 11:6
52. Jeremiah 33:3
53. I Samuel 15
54. II Samuel 12:13 & Psalm 51
55. Jeremiah 29:11
56. Psalm 119:78 & I Peter 2:2
57. I Corinthians 13 & Ephesians 6:10 16
58. Exodus 16:13–19 & Joshua 1:11 & 5:12
59. James 1:23
60. I Samuel 15: 22&23
61. Ephesians 4:32
62. Matthew 18:21–35
63. Matthew 6:9–13
64. John 14:6 & Acts 4:12
65. Matthew 18:21–35
66. This is seen numerous times throughout scripture, Jacob & Esau, Moses & Pharoah, the pagan nations being used to discipline the nation of Israel and many more.
67. Psalm 13
68. Philippians 4:11&12
69. Hebrews 13:5
70. Psalm 100:4
71. Hebrew 13:15
72. Matthew 5:45
73. Proverbs 3:19

74. Proverbs 13:20
75. Colossians 3:2
76. Proverbs 3:14 & 8:17
77. James 1:5
78. I Corinthians 12:8
79. Hebrews 12:7
80. II Peter 1:3
81. Luke 6:12
82. Luke 11:1
83. Mark 3:20
84. Mark 1:35
85. Ephesians 6:10–16
86. 1 Peter 5:8
87. Galatians 5:22&23
88. Ephesians 5:25
89. Matthew 5:28
90. Ephesians 5:33
91. Matthew 5:43&44
92. Luke 9:23
93. Psalm 16:11; 21:6; 140:13 & Luke 5:1 & 10:39
94. This is based on a Bible principle. Throughout scripture and through the present, the Father never forces us to do His will. Combine this knowledge with the Holy Spirit power of which I have already referenced and this conclusion is drawn.
95. Matthew 14:23–36
96. I Corinthians 13:12
97. Hebrews 12:1
98. Exodus 23: 29–33
99. I John 4:4

100. Psalm 55:19; Malachi 3:6; Hebrew 13:8
101. II Timothy 2:22
102. Philippians 4:13
103. I Corinthians 12:7
104. John 3:3 & II Peter 1:3
105. Romans 14:7
106. John 17:4
107. Matthew 6:33 & 34
108. Exodus 3:14
109. Philippians 4:4
110. Daniel 3
111. Philippians 4:13
112. Exodus 14 & Joshua 3
113. I Thessalonians 5:18
114. Daniel 3:25
115. II Corinthians 1:4–7
116. Psalm 150:6
117. Hebrews 11:16
118. Hebrews 11:3
119. Matthew 25:23